Instant CASH Flow!

By **T.J. Rohleder**
(a.k.a "The Blue Jeans Millionaire")

Other Great Titles from T.J. Rohleder:

Ruthless Marketing Secrets (Series)
The 2-Step Marketing Secret That Never Fails
Stealth Marketing
The Power of Hype
3 Steps to Instant Profits
Money Machine
The Blue Jeans Millionaire
How to Turn Your Kitchen or Spare Bedroom into a Cash Machine
The Black Book of Marketing Secrets (Series)
The Ultimate Wealth-Maker
Four Magical Secrets to Building a Fabulous Fortune
The Ruthless Marketing Attack
How to Get Super Rich in the Opportunity Market
$60,000.00 in 90 Days
How to Start Your Own Million Dollar Business
Fast Track to Riches
Five Secrets That Will Triple Your Profits
Ruthless Copywriting Strategies
25 Direct Mail Success Secrets That Can Make You Rich
Ruthless Marketing
24 Simple and Easy Ways to Get Rich Quick
How to Create a Hot Selling Internet Product in One Day
50 in 50
Secrets of the Blue Jeans Millionaire
Shortcut Secrets to Creating High-Profit Products
Foolproof Secrets of Sucessful Millionaires
How to Make Millions While Sitting on Your Ass
500 Ways to Get More People to Give You More Money

Printed in the United States of America. For information address: M.O.R.E. Incorporated, 305 East Main Street, Goessel, Kansas 67053-0198.

FIRST EDITION

ISBN 1-933356-99-5

TABLE OF CONTENTS

INTRODUCTION:

By T.J. Rohleder

Thank you for purchasing this book and TAKING THE TIME to go through it. As you'll see—this can be one of the SMARTEST DECISIONS you'll ever make because it will give you a very powerful competitive advantage in your marketplace.

IT'S TRUE! This book contains some of my greatest marketing secrets that give you the awesome power to attract and retain the largest percentage of the very best clients and customers in your market. Now you will have the power to get even more of these people to come to you, instead of your competition!

Does the idea of getting the VERY BEST clients and customers in your market to come to YOU instead of all of your competitors excite you? IF SO—GREAT! Keep this excitement as you go through this book! Plus, take advantage of my very special FREE GIFT that I'll tell you about in a minute! As you'll see, this gives you 6,159 of my all-time-greatest marketing secrets that you can use to find, get, and keep MORE of the very best customers and clients in your marketplace! So with all this said...

Here's What You'll Discover In This Book

This book gives you some of my most powerful marketing

secrets for attracting and retaining the very best customers and clients in your market. The first chapter is also the title of this book. It gives you THE 7-STEP FORMULA to writing a hard-hitting sales letter. As you'll see, **this gives you the power to build your business with DIRECT MAIL MARKETING.** This can give you THE INSTANT CASH FLOW you need RIGHT NOW!

Direct Mail is the #1 marketing method that I've used to build my own business. It's generated tens of millions of dollars worth of sales for me and that's how I know for a fact that it can generate a HUGE FORTUNE for you!

So please take the time to go over Chapter One and get this simple, but totally proven FORMULA for writing a sales letter that can get more cash flowing into your business—starting now! **Then enjoy all of the other secrets you'll discover in the remaining chapters.** And REMEMBER THIS: In today's overcrowded and over-competitive marketplace, the individual or company who is the VERY BEST MARKETER is the one that comes out on top! Having the very best product or service is NOT ENOUGH... You must know all you can about all of the ways to find, get, and keep MORE of the very best customers and clients in your marketplace. Do this and you'll have a MAJOR ADVANTAGE that can be worth huge sums of money!

So take the time to go over this book and DISCOVER some of my most powerful and proven marketing methods that can let you ATTRACT and RETAIN the largest number of the very best customers and clients in your marketplace. And then take advantage of...

My FREE business-building gift!

Yes, I have a gift waiting for you that can DRAMATICALLY INCREASE YOUR SALES AND PROFITS! Here's what it's all about: I spent TEN FULL YEARS writing down all of the greatest marketing and success secrets I discovered during that time period. Each day, I took a few notes and at the end of a decade, I had a GIANT LIST of 6,159 powerful secrets! This list is ALMOST 1,000 PAGES of hardcore money-making ideas and strategies!** **Best of all, this massive collection is now YOURS ABSOLUTELY FREE!** Just go to: www.6159FreeSecrets.com and get it NOW! As you'll see, this complete collection of 6,159 of my greatest marketing and success secrets, far more valuable than those you can buy from others for $495 to $997, is absolutely **FREE.** No cost, no obligation.

Why am I giving away this GIANT COLLECTION of secrets, that took ONE DECADE to discover and compile, FOR FREE? That's simple: I believe many of the people who receive these 6,159 secrets in this huge 955 page PDF document will want to obtain some of our other books and audio programs and participate in our special COACHING PROGRAMS. However, you are NOT obligated to buy anything—now or ever.

I know you're serious about making more money or you wouldn't be reading this. So go to: www.6159FreeSecrets.com and get this complete collection of 6,159 of my greatest marketing and success secrets right now! **You'll get this GREAT FREE GIFT in the next few minutes, just for letting me add you to my Client mailing list,** and I'll stay in CLOSE

TOUCH with you... and do all I can to help you make even more money with my proven marketing strategies and methods.

So with all this said, let's begin…

** WARNING: This complete collection of 6,159 marketing and success secrets contains MANY CONTROVERSIAL ideas and methods. Also, it was originally written for MY EYES ONLY and for a few VERY CLOSE FRIENDS. Therefore, the language is X-RATED in some places [I got VERY EXCITED when I wrote many of these ideas and used VERY FOUL LANGUAGE to get my ideas across!] so 'IF' you are EASILY OFFENDED or do NOT want to read anything OFFENSIVE, then please do both of us a favor and DO NOT go to my website and download this FREE gift. THANK YOU for your understanding.

CHAPTER ONE

How to write a powerful, hard-hitting sales letter:

1. Start with a big promise.
2. Paint the picture.
3. Give them proof.
4. Tell them <u>why</u> it's unique.
5. Close your argument by telling them why they must act now!
6. Make them a very special offer <u>if</u> they respond now!
7. End with a reminder of the promise — summary of offer — and STRONG call for action!

That's it! This is the blueprint or schematic of a sales letter — from start to finish.

Learn to Write Powerful, Hard-Hitting Sales Letters

A lot of people know our story. They know that when we first met Russ von Hoelscher, we were six months into the business, and we were bringing in about $16,000 a month. To us, that was all the money in the world! Then we met Russ, and we went from $16,000 a month to almost $100,000 a *week* within nine months. Now, that's just total revenue, not profits. But think about that leap: from about $500 a day to almost $15,000 a day. So people want to know what it was that Russ did for us, and the truth is, he did a lot of things for us. **But the *main* thing he did was that he got us started with direct mail. Now, some people call it "junk mail." We don't. We treasure it.**

So what *is* direct mail, exactly? Some people think it's just advertising, but to us it's not advertising at all. **The way we think about it, direct mail is a way to put a sales presentation into an envelope. It's salesmanship in print.** It's taking everything you would normally use in a face-to-face selling environment, and putting it into an envelope. When we mail out 100,000 direct mail letters, we think of them as 100,000 salespeople who never call in sick. They're never late to work. They always do their jobs.

Direct mail pieces are written using easily-learned formulas, and in this chapter, **I'll give you a seven-step**

formula for writing a winning sales letter for a direct mail packet. It's like a recipe for a cake. Even if you're not a master chef, if you follow that cake recipe, chances are you're create a cake that's worth eating. **We call this a blueprint or a schematic of a sales letter, from start to finish.**

The FIRST STEP is to start with a big promise; and the bigger and bolder the promise, the better. For example, in the initial sales material we're developing for our new direct pay system, the biggest promise is the chance to get paid directly. The money bypasses the company and goes straight to you. That's the big promise we start with, and if you know the business opportunity market at all, you'll know it's a pretty big one indeed. **Then NUMBER TWO, you paint the picture.** This involves trying to personalize that promise and making it real to the reader. **You're trying to get them to step into the picture.**

NUMBER THREE, you give them proof. People are so skeptical these days, and that skepticism is part of a growing trend. **Therefore, you have to give them some proof as to why you can actually fulfill on this particular promise. NUMBER FOUR, you have to tell people why what you're offering is unique, why it's different.** That's what people are looking for: things that are different. Simultaneously, it needs to be something similar to what they've bought before... and yes, I realizes that this idea will drive some people crazy. **It has to be the same and different at the same time; it has to be familiar, but have some points of uniqueness that make it stand out.**

NUMBER FIVE: you close your argument by telling them why they have to take action now, because if you don't give people a strong, compelling reason to act immediately, they won't. **Then, in step NUMBER SIX, you make them a special offer if they *do* respond now.** Give them something really nice that pushes them over the edge, so to speak, that helps them make a decision to go ahead and take advantage of what you're offering. **And finally, with NUMBER SEVEN, you end the letter with a reminder of the promise that you made in the beginning, a summarization of the entire offer, and a strong call to action at the end.** That's an effective seven-step blueprint, a formula of the kind that people who write sales letters for a living tend to follow.

Incidentally: I firmly believe that if you're interested in getting rich with direct mail, **you should send for as much direct mail as you can, and study it. That way you can try to determine the common denominators.** I just gave you a seven-step formula, and you'll find those key ideas in every successful direct mail packet. You'll also find those key ideas in any sales presentation. It's all about salesmanship. **It's about proving to people, beyond any doubt, that what you have to offer them is worth more than the money you're asking for in return.**

You're building a case. You're making them a bold promise, something that is attractive to them, and then you're showing them why it's in their best interests to go ahead and take action. Think about it. Anybody can just say, "Hey! This is the greatest thing on Earth!", but nobody is going to believe them. **You've got to prove, beyond any doubt that people have, that what you have is real, that it's solid, it's different, and it really does give them what they want.** You need to cover every possible objection, every possible doubt, every possible concern that somebody might have, while covering every possible benefit.

There are people out there making millions of dollars with direct mail—and it's just good old-fashioned salesmanship, in an envelope. If you look at the so-called "junk mail" you're getting, the good stuff, you'll see this formula pretty clearly, and you'll be able to pick out the different parts. I would encourage you to pay close attention to that as you're trying to learn direct mail and become an expert marketer. Grab as many sales letters as you can handle and study them. **As you read through the offer, look for these seven items, and mark them. Eventually, it will all become second nature.**

You see, we don't really worry about such things her at M.O.R.E., Inc., at least not consciously. We're to the part where we're not actively thinking about them. We don't look at a sales letter and go, "Okay... we need to start with a big promise," and then write it and check it off the list, and go on to number two. It's really just second nature by now. We know the important parts of a sales letter, and so we just write knowing these parts. **But when getting started, the best way to figure all this out is to see where these parts fit in other people's sales copy.** So grab some sales letters... and **remember, they have to be good ones.** You see a lot of junk out there, a lot of crap that looks like glorified fliers or posters. They don't use good sales copy, and they don't use the right formulas... and those things usually don't get a good response.

Study only the good models that are being mailed to you. Look at the invitations and offers that we send to you, and try to pick these sales letters apart. Grab seven different colors of highlighter, one for each of the seven points in this formula, and highlight the points, or circle them as you see them. **Look for the big promise at the beginning; that's probably going to be the headline.** Generally speaking, with our offers, the headline takes the form of a big, bold promise. **And then, as you look through the letter, you'll see us painting a big picture—usually in the form of a story,** which you'll see pretty early on. It could be a story about something that happened to us. It could be just a metaphor—a made-up story imagining what life would be like in a certain scenario in which the reader receives the benefits of what we're offering. **We're putting together a visual or a mental picture of what they're reading on the paper.**

That's the big picture of what you want them to get. You've made a big, bold promise in the headline. **There's something that jumps out and grabs their attention—and in the big picture is the pre-story.** Maybe you see these over the first page or two. Sometimes, if it's a long sales letter, it'll take several pages. But it's developing the story: you're telling them, "Here's what I'm going to tell you as you read my sales copy. I'm going to offer you this item. I'm going to tell you what I want you to do or what I want you to imagine your life being like after you've received the benefit I just promised you in my headline."

People have to see themselves benefiting from your product. This is true whether you're selling to the opportunity market, or if you have a diet pill that will help people lose weight. As they read your offer, they're going to be skeptical no matter what the product is, no matter what the offer is. **You're making them a big, bold guarantee if you're using the right**

formula here, and so you have to prove it to them. Proof can come in the form of testimonials. It can come from you just showing them how it's possible. There are all different kinds of things you can do to include proof—but **you do want to prove to them early on that what you're saying is believable, and show them why they should trust you.** Prove that you've got the evidence to back it up: your claim is validated by this, that, or the other. Go into the proof to verify that what you're saying is true.

No matter how much people like what you write, no matter what you're selling or who you're selling to: when people read your sales copy, they're immediately skeptical. For example: Chris Lakey recently had a door-to-door salesman come by his house, which is strange because it doesn't happen very often anymore, and the guy was selling a household cleaner in a bottle. Now, Chris tells me it wasn't much bigger than a 20 ounce bottle of water—it may have been as much as 30 ounces—and he was selling it for about $40. He was a good salesman, and like me, Chris likes to listen to salespeople pitch their products, so he took the time to hear what the guy had to say.

So Chris opened the door, and salesman introduced himself. And then he said what he was doing there, and asked, "Do you mind if I clean your front door here?" So he cleaned the glass in Chris's front door, which was pretty clean anyway; Chris had just moved in a few months before. Then he showed Chris how when you wiped your finger on it, it didn't leave fingerprints, because the cleaner was fingerprint-proof. And then he went out to Chris's car and cleaned the bumper a little bit and moved on to the windshield, and this whole time Chris was thinking, "I'm seeing proof that what he's telling me is true. **He's showing me that his product really does what he's telling me." And yet Chris was also thinking, "Yeah, right." He was skeptical.**

Well, Chris didn't end up buying a bottle of the cleaner, but he thanked the guy for coming by and for being brave enough to be out there doing door-to-door sales. **There he was, showing Chris visible proof that what he was telling him about his product was accurate.** I don't think there's any way he could have been making it do anything that it wasn't going to do later. He even cleaned Chris's driveway with a toothbrush. He said, "See this water stain here?" So he was down there scrubbing and he was sweating. It was a hot day, so he was sweating like crazy, and he apologized for being all sweaty. But there he was, showing Chris physically that his product worked. I mean, we talk about selling by mail or selling in a sales letter... and here's this guy at Chris's door showing him visible proof of his product's effectiveness.

Meanwhile, Chris is standing there being skeptical, thinking, *There's got to be a catch. Something isn't right here. This product can't be worth $40.* That's justifiable; he could probably buy a bottle of cleaner that size at Wal-Mart for four or five bucks, and this guy was selling one for $40. Chris was seeing visible proof of his claims; it was true. He believed it; he was seeing it, and he couldn't doubt it. **And yet he was *skeptical,* and he didn't end up buying.** That's something you deal with whenever you sell something, no matter how you're selling it, no matter what it is. **People have to have proof; and the more proof you can give them, the more likely you are to**

make a sale. So giving them proof is an important step. Why is it unique? What makes this different from anything else?

This salesman who came to Chris's door did a good job of that. Why was this $40 bottle of cleaner more unique, better than the $5 bottle you could buy at Wal-Mart? Well, he was telling Chris things like the fact that it doesn't smear. You know, if you clean your bathroom mirror, your kids will probably come along and smudge it up with their fingerprints in just a few minutes. Chris has a big, double glass sliding door leading to his patio, and he's also got five kids; so that glass door has fingerprints all over it all the time. And so as he was hearing the guy tell him about this, he was thinking the whole time, "Man, my wife would love this." He still didn't buy, but it's a unique product with proof of its benefits. You're not going to get those benefits by buying something over-the-counter at your local Wal-Mart, and this fellow was doing a good job of telling Chris why this product was unique.

That's an important step. **Why is *this* different than anything else you can get in the marketplace?** If you're selling the same widget that anyone can get at Wal-Mart, you're going to have a hard time competing, because Wal-Mart is probably buying a million of those widgets, and you're only buying a few at a time. **And you *can't* compete on price; that's always a mistake,** barring the occasional special sale. **You've got to offer something else.** So why is your experience unique?

Recently, we were chatting with our good friend Jeff Gardner about some of his early experiences as a distributor for a product of ours called 60 Minute Riches. He took off like a rocket with that program, making money hand over fist, just going like gangbusters! Now, we had some distributors who weren't doing very well at all; they weren't selling anything. I suspect that most of them probably weren't trying that hard. And here Jeff was, thrilled and making a lot of money selling the very same program. One of the things that he would happily share about his success was that he didn't just do what everybody else was doing. **He added some free gifts to the offer on his own, he reworked the sales copy a little, and he added his own personal flavor to the sales process. He put some of his own story in there. He took what everybody else was a distributor for, and made it unique and attractive.**

That's what separated what he was doing from everybody else, and you see this in all successful offers. **Part of the story is telling people why what you're offering them is a unique experience, something they're not going to get by doing business with other people. Then, as you start to wrap up your sales copy, you close your argument by telling them why they need to act right now.** This is part of your offer, an incentive to get them to respond right away. If they respond *now* they will get *these* bonus gifts. If they act fast they will get *this* discount. Whatever your offer is, it's giving them a reason to do business with you immediately... because if they wait, they might wait forever. If you have a great product and all it takes to sell it is to say, "Hey, I've got this product, here's how much it costs," and you sit on a street corner, you'll get some sales. But if you have a direct mail offer, and all you do is tell them that you have a product and here's how much it costs, all in plain words on one piece of paper, it's just a boring statement of fact: *I have this product for sale, and here's how much you can buy it for.*

If you do that, a few people will respond—those who, for whatever reason, are extremely interested in that product at that moment will send their order in. Don't count on many orders happening, though, because **people typically don't respond even if you give them a good reason to.** Just having the product doesn't get you orders. **No, you need to put together an offer, something that makes people want to order it today.** And there are all kinds of offers you can make: buy one get one free, everything is half off today, here's a free gift or two. It all depends on what your marketplace is—whether you're a retail store, or whether you're selling a business opportunity by mail. **You want to package your offer together in such a way that it makes them want to respond right now, and a time sensitive offer always works for that.** You can tell them, "Respond within the next 24 hours, and get these free gifts." Or, "Our product will be launching on this date and you need to get your order in, in advance." It's up to you to determine why they need to take action today.

And then the last thing: end with a reminder of the promise. Summarize the offer so that you're book-ending the promise. **You started with a big bold promise—usually in your headline—and you end with a reminder of that promise.** There at the end, you're reminding them of the benefit that you promised them, the guarantee you made them, and then you couple it with a strong call to action. "Do this now!" ***Tell* people what to do.** People generally do what they're told to, and in general, **people *need* to be told what to do.** So if you tell them what to do in your copy, and tell them exactly how to do it, people will generally follow suit. **If you have a strong offer, if it's something they want to respond to, they'll follow**

your instructions.

So tell them how to do it. Tell them that the big, bold promise you made is only minutes away. All they have to do is call this toll free number, and they'll be getting it in the mail. This package will arrive, and it will solve all their problems. **Whatever the promise you've made to them, remind them that all they have to do to take advantage of the solution is to take action.** All they have to do is send in the form, respond to your offer, and the relief from whatever pain they're in is moments away.

So that's the blueprint; and again, I encourage you to start looking at sales copy in a different way. Begin by looking closely at the offers you receive in the mail. Start to analyze them with these seven things in mind. Go through and circle the points that fall into each of these categories, and then number them out according to the category. Any time you see a big bold promise, especially at the front of the letter, in the first page or so, that's a number one. Any time you see proof, write a number three next to it. Any time you see that person painting a picture, write a number two. Anytime you see a close, a response mechanism of some kind, write a number six. You'll start to see how the marketers craft their offers. You can do the same thing. **Write your own sales copy using that same formula!**

The more you look at modern direct mail marketing, the more common denominators you'll see. And let me point something out: we don't necessarily sell products and services in this business. **What we really sell are offers.** I was in the business for seven or eight years before I really figured that out. Now, what *are* offers? **An offer is just what its name suggests:**

all the things you're going to give someone in exchange for their money. Sure, it represents the product or service that you sell, but it's also all the extra bonuses and special incentives. Someone asked me recently regarding an offer, "Is that the best you can do?" No! We've got a special offer for you. Here's what we're going to do to top that. If you take action today, here's what else we're going to give you. **It's a special offer, and that's really what we sell. And direct mail is such a fun way to make money!**

CHAPTER TWO

The power of the 5 A.M. Club:

- ☆ Force yourself to get out of bed before you want to — and put on a big pot of strong black coffee. — Pull out some paper and pens and start writing!
- ☆ Ideas <u>will</u> come to you and through you — that you would <u>never</u> have discovered <u>if</u> you stayed in bed!

There is a magic at work here that's hard to explain! You must experience it — <u>before</u> you can believe it!

INSTANT CASH FLOW!

The Power of the 5:00 AM Club

The 5:00 AM Club is a special club; I've been a member for years. I'm sure there are many hundreds of thousands of members, although we don't know each other; it's a funny club that way. **Here's how it works: you force yourself to get out of bed before you *want* to get out of bed.** For me, it's around 5:00 or 5:30 in the morning. I'd much rather stay in bed with my dear wife, especially in the winter, where it's all nice and warm. But you do get up, you put on a big pot of strong black coffee, you pull out some paper and some pens or a laptop computer, and you get to work.

The principle is this: You sit down and brainstorm, and ideas will come to you that I'm convinced you would never have discovered had you stayed in bed. That's the 5:00 AM Club. There's a magic at work here; it's hard to explain, and yet I've experienced it so many times it doesn't even surprise me anymore. In fact, I kind of expect it now. I can't always make that magic happen, but I can create the situations that cause it to show up whenever it's ready to. And I realize that you really have to experience this before you can believe it.

Most people know that if they come up with the right combination of ideas, they could go out there and make millions of dollars. All it takes is presenting those ideas in the right way to the right people, and the money could come flowing in so fast that you wouldn't know how to intelligently spend it all. It's happened to me, and it's happened to a lot of other people. **And yet, most entrepreneurs and business owners have never spent any time really thinking it through**—thinking about where the ideas come from, how to develop them, how to get more of those ideas and, most importantly, how to get the best ideas, the ones that are going to make the most impact and turn everything around.

Here's an overall principle that I'd like you to memorize. It's just a simple quote, but there's a great amount of truth to it: **"You go as far as you can see, and when you get there, you can see even farther."** Oftentimes, people are confused; they want those million dollar ideas, because they know that if they just get one or two, it could turn everything around for them. But where *are* those multimillion dollar ideas? **Well, they come from hard work, from moving forward, from getting involved in a whole bunch of different projects.** When I talk about how the 5:00 AM Club triggers ideas that would never have come had you not forced yourself to get out of bed, **I'm talking about getting up and starting to *work*.**

I'm talking about creative kinds of work, things that involve marketing. It's not work in a traditional sense; it's a creative, artistic kind of fun. It's still confusing and frustrating sometimes, and often very challenging. Nobody has it all figured out. **But here's the thing: if you get up and keep working on different promotions and projects designed to get more people to give you more money, the ideas will come to you, sometimes in a flash.** If you don't write them down, you'll forget them.

I've already talked about how I'll sometimes sit in the shower in the morning and think for a long time. It's not my only secret for coming up with really creative ideas, but it works. I get up, pour myself a cup of coffee, then sit down in the shower and let the hot water and the caffeine do their magic. Sometimes, if I'm really confused and frustrated, I'll just sit in the shower until I get an idea. It may take ten minutes, or it may take an hour. In the meantime, I'm going down, making more coffee, going back upstairs and sitting in the shower. **There's something about that hot water that helps—and there's been some scientific evidence to support this, too, so it's not nearly as crazy as you might think.** And of course, the caffeine is certainly a jump start to my brain.

I always have a handful of projects going at all once; usually, I'm juggling four or five in various stages of completion. **Some have tighter deadlines than others, and as the deadlines approach and the pressure starts mounting, that's when a lot of the ideas just bubble up to the surface.** For example: this past Friday I spent the entire day finishing a boring job, polishing off a long form sales letter. It's not difficult work; it's just detailed typing work, and it takes hours. I hate having to sit on my butt for hours in front of a computer; I absolutely hate it. And yet I got through it, I got it done; and I sent it in an email to the graphic artist on Friday. And then, on Saturday morning, I was upstairs at 5:30 or 6:00 in the morning, drinking my coffee in the shower, thinking about ideas, thinking about where to take this thing next, about priorities.

I was sweating about it, so to speak. I was stressing out a little bit, I was frustrated, I was confused, I was trying to sort it all out, and all of a sudden, I got an idea! That led to another idea, which led to another idea, and *boom*! A whole new direction emerged, from things that I wasn't really even thinking about initially. It just all came together for me. Now we're running with it... and things like this happen all the time. Where were these ideas that I got in the shower about 60 or 70 hours ago? Where was that idea last week? **The answer is, that new idea came from a culmination of a whole lot of other older ideas that we were already working on.**

That's one big point I want to make here. I've got all kinds of things going on, at various stages of completion. But the ones that are completed are all things that can be revamped, and then there are all kinds of pressures that come from commitments that we've made and plans that we're working on. There are all these pressures and problems floating around, like little jigsaw pieces. **The magic that comes into play here is the creativity that links all these pieces together.** That's what creativity is, they say. In order to get these ideas, though, you have all the pieces floating around that you *can* link together. **So, my recommendation is to stay involved in as many things as you can. Keep the pressure on, and then make time to be creative every day.** It doesn't have to be at five in the morning. Maybe you're a late night person. A lot of creative people work late nights. For whatever reason, they don't want to get up early in the morning; some of them like sleeping in. But they burn that midnight oil.

Another point: think on paper, because ideas will escape you if you don't record them. Plus, you have to allow yourself plenty of time to be creative. Creativity is work. A lot of people don't think of it like that, because it's not work in a traditional sense. It can be fun—but again, it can also be very frustrating and confusing. I've got a good friend whom I turned on to marketing about nine years ago. I gave him all these tapes, and he was starting to get really excited about it. Then, after the excitement wore off, he told me he stopped subjecting himself to all these ideas and such, and I asked him why. He said, "It got so frustrating and confusing to me." Well, join the crowd! **Frustration and confusion is all part of the process, and it *is* a process.** Don't let anybody ever fool you into thinking it isn't. **It's a process where you have to allow yourself time to be creative, so more ideas lead to more ideas, and more ideas lead to *better* ideas.**

You've also got to focus on your customers, thinking about the things that they want the most, what they're buying the most of, and what other people are promoting to them that they're the most excited about. That's also when you'll get some of your best ideas. **It's about finding a way to combine the things that have worked the best for you in the past; or, if you don't have things that have worked the best for you in the past, things that are working well for the main competitors in your market.**

Look at this as a lifestyle. It's not a job. A job is something you punch in and out of; you put in your time, and you go home. This is a way of life. It's a creative process; you're hunting these ideas down. And whether it's 5:00 o'clock in the morning, or 3:00 o'clock in the morning, or 1:00 o'clock in the morning, you've got to allow yourself the time to think and dream and create and work.

Sometimes your best ideas come when you're in the thick of another job. Sometimes the ideas come when you want to avoid a job you're working on, so you come up with some breakthrough ideas in another area. **However it happens, you have to be ready for it.** Again, it is a process, and you get better as you go along—just like when you're strengthening muscles in a gym. If you go to the gym every day for a couple of hours, it's only a matter of time before you're going to have a hard body. It's the same thing with being creative.

This is one of those foundational principles of successful entrepreneurship, and I think it transcends the mail marketing industry and niche markets. It's an important strategy to think about if you're dedicated to success. Now, I've already alluded to the fact that this could be the 5:00 AM Club for you, or it could be the 2:00 AM Club, or the 11:00 PM Club, or any other time, depending on how your day's regular schedule goes. If you're a budding entrepreneur who happens to work the night shift, and you normally sleep all day, then maybe your 5:00 AM is actually 5:00 PM, and you're getting up then instead of at 6:00 PM or 7:00 PM. **The time isn't really as important as the concept here, which is forcing yourself to spend time doing something proactive for your business. The ideas will flow from that.**

Another thing about the 5:00 AM Club is that it's all about what you do with your time. Most people are asleep at 5:00 AM, which is why I've committed to getting up at 5:00 AM. Well, what next? Let's say I go sit on the couch and turn on the television and see that there's nothing on. So I got to the refrigerator and get some breakfast. Pretty soon it's seven o'clock, when most people would normally get up anyway, and I go about my day. Well, that's not what the 5:00 AM Club was designed to be all about. **If you just fritter your time away, or maybe do some chores around the house—if you do any other things besides business—you're not really going to get the benefit from the 5:00 AM Club concept, are you?**

The important thing is what you do with your time, not so much that you've *made* the time. Ask yourself: what are you trying to accomplish? Well, I would hope that you spend that time worrying about all the ways to bring in more sales, how to do more business with your existing customers, coming up with new ideas for products and services, new ways to serve your marketplace and earn a profit doing it. How do you get there? What can you do that actually makes this special time productive? Again, you need to start with an intimate knowledge of your marketplace. **Spend a little bit of time first figuring out who you're selling to. Once you know that, you can make the 5:00 AM Club insanely productive.**

So, you get up early in the morning, or you stay up late at night, and think about how to serve your marketplace. Now, you may say, "I'm an entrepreneur; I don't have a job other than being an entrepreneur," or "I'm retired. This is my passion, this is something I do in my spare time, but I'm pretty much dedicated to it and I can do it all day. I can do it any time I want. So why would I want to get up early in the morning? I like sleeping!" **The answer is that it's focused time.** Other times of the day, you have to spend time with your family, and do things to maintain your household.

Chris Lakey, for example, has six kids at home—and if any

of them are awake while he's home, he's busy doing stuff with them. It's difficult for him to do anything else. One day last week, Chris was feeling poorly, and he was here in the office. He joked to me that he was probably better off here than at home, where he'd have his kids fighting on his lap, needing attention. Whereas at the office, he could be at least semi-productive instead trying to fend off six kids! That's what happens when you have children at home. Even if they're out of the house, you've got a spouse vying for your attention, and of course they *deserve* a certain level of attention!

And you also have the other things that happen on a daily basis: people calling, the phone ringing, your email going crazy, the TV on in the background. **There are all these distractions that happen during the course of a regular day, and what that ends up meaning is that your focused time gets greatly reduced.** You may squeeze in five minutes here, or 10 minutes there. **You may have some time where you can devote to doing things, but it's not focused, high-quality time.**

So let's say you know that your house is going to be a hustle and a bustle by 7:00 AM, so you get up at 5:00 AM. **You can have two hours of uninterrupted time, where you're focused on serving your customers by developing products and services, finding ways to extract more money from your marketplace.** And you don't have to worry about the phone ringing, because who's going to call you at 5:30 in the morning? Your phone is quiet, there's nobody asking you to make them breakfast, there's no one knocking at the door—so you could get some quality time in. And it's the same thing with 11:00 PM, or whatever. Unlike me, Chris tends to have his best quiet time after everybody's in bed in the evening, and he's not necessarily a morning person anyway. His wife is, so she goes to bed a little before Chris, and is up before him in the morning. He usually stays up later than her in the evening, and that's the quiet time for him.

That's really the big benefit of the 5:00 AM Club. **It's focused energy, a predetermined block of time where you're going to be committed to working on your business.** You're going to be dedicated to spending time thinking about all the ways you can serve your marketplace and make a profit. **And remember, it's not the time of day that matters; it's that you take the time, and do it consistently at the same time every day so you can plan for it.** If you have a habit of getting up every day at 5:00 AM, you're going to make sure that nothing stops you. Your alarm is going to be set every day.

If you just say, "I'm dedicated to spending two hours with my business every day," well, some days you wake up and you don't feel like it, and you hit the snooze button. Other days, you just don't do it for whatever reason. So by committing a time where you do it every day, you're going to be more dedicated to it. And you'll find that you do it because you don't want to be disappointed when you're unable to do it. **The 5:00 AM club is an important tool you can use to discipline yourself in order to be successful in your business. It's mostly about dedication and commitment to the process, and to the goal of doing better in your business.**

And "commitment" is a powerful word here, because when you study the lives of the most successful people, you'll find they went through a ton of different challenges and adversities getting there. There were many times they could have (and maybe should have) quit, and yet they didn't, because they were deeply committed to their dreams. **They realized what you should realize: that all the ideas and money that you're looking for are out there, right now, if you'll just make that commitment.**

Three Proven Ways To Make Money:

1. Do something nobody wants to do.

2. Do stuff others cannot be bothered to do — or would rather not do.

3. Do something you're great at that others are terrible at!!

The Three Proven Ways to Make Money

When you get right down to it, there are just three proven ways to make money. **The first is to do something that nobody else wants to do. The second is to do things that other people can't be bothered to do. The third is to do something that you're great at, and that others are terrible at.** It's possible to do something that fits all three categories... but to clarify things, let's look at specific examples of each.

I want to start with the third item first, because in my opinion, **that's where all the happiness is: when you can find something that you're really, really good at that other people struggle with—so much so that they're willing to pay you a lot of money to do it.** That should always be your end goal. **Now, here's the entire secret to number three: to get really good at something might take you years.** That's really all there is to it. People are usually bad at things just because they don't put the kind of time, effort, energy, dedication, passion and commitment into them that they require; that's all.

Case in point: anytime Chris Lakey and I wanted to, we could run ads on the Internet and in the trade journals to sell our copywriting services. Writing decent copy is a highly specialized skill that other people will pay a lot of money for, and quite frankly, it's taken us many years to get good at it. I'm not saying that we're the greatest in the world —in fact, I'm not even saying that there's not plenty of room for improvement, or that we're not going to continue to get better. **But what I *am* saying is that it's taken us thousands of hours to get to the point where we're very good at copywriting.** That's the reason why so many people *aren't* good at it. They try writing copy, and they fail at it; so they give it up in frustration and hire freelance copywriters, paying them a lot of money do the job for them.

Now, maybe I'm just a slow learner, **but it was *eight years* before I was happy with my proficiency as a copywriter.** That's a long time—so long that most people would give up before they got to that point. During that whole time I was working hard on it, but it was a full eight years before I was skilled enough to write a good control piece for use in new customer acquisition. **Prior to that, my sales letters were good enough to draw people in, so I was writing sales letters, developing existing campaigns and so forth;** I was good enough to sell stuff to existing customers, which isn't a bad place to be in. But when it came to selling stuff to people outside our customer database, I just didn't have the skills. I hadn't done it for long enough, and just wasn't good enough yet.

So that's category number three: doing something that you're really good at that others are terrible at. **The secret to achieving this is simply to put in the necessary time and effort.** From the very first moment I found out about copywriting, I wanted to learn how to do it... but at the beginning, my efforts sucked. I'll never forget the time I spent several weeks writing a full page ad before showing it to Russ von Hoelscher, our mentor. I wanted him to tweak it, that's all. He'd been working with us for just six months at that point, and he said: "Why didn't you just let me write it for you?" I told him I didn't want to; I wanted to learn how to do it myself. Then, when I was finally done, he proceeded to fix it—and made it a lot better. It was because of his changes, especially the killer headline he wrote, that the ad worked as well as it did.

But the point is, I wanted to learn how to do this, so I started working on that end of things. It took me many years to get good at it, and I think that's the norm rather than the exception. **When someone is the best at whatever it is that they do, it's because it took them years to get to that point**—and the casual observer just doesn't realize that, often because the expert doesn't want them to think about the amount of time and work, effort and energy that they had to put into their specialty. They want you to think that they're somehow blessed with a natural ability, that they have some God-given gift that *you* weren't born with. **The more they can make you feel they have special powers, the more you're willing to pay them.**

I do think that there are some people who are naturally gifted... but I also think that there are a lot more people who make it to the top by working their way there. They're very good at what they do, and they can charge a lot of money for it. **They've learned to be good at it because, in most cases, they really enjoy it.** If you strive to get to that place, you'll not only be paid tremendous amounts of money for what you do, but you'll also be very fulfilled at the same time. "Heaven on Earth" is what I call it.

Now, let's talk about the other two ways to make money. **The first is do something nobody wants to do, and the second one is do something that others can't be bothered to do.**

Here's a good example of both. About 30 years ago, I read a story in the newspaper about a company in Denver that had 50 independent contractors... and the owner was making over $100,000 a year, simply by doing something that most people are glad to let other people do for them. The name of his company was Pooper Scoopers. That's right, Pooper Scoopers. This guy's company specialized in picking up dog poop in people's yards. They even had special services in case the dog got sick and threw up all over your carpet, or pooped all over your rug. They would come in and take care of the mess for you. All kinds of people called Pooper Scoopers, just so they could avoid cleaning up after their pets. They even had little kids who were giving up parts of their allowances to hire Pooper Scoopers!

Now, on the more practical side, my best friend owns a pest control business. **They do over a million dollars a year, and basically all they do is spray for bugs.** That's something *anybody* can do, and it doesn't cost a lot of money to get started. You just need one of those pump-up cans and some bug poison, and you can go into people's houses and spray. **But it's something that people would rather not do themselves, so they hire companies like my friend's.** And she charges a lot of money, too! She's not one of those low-ball companies; she charges premium prices, because people really, really hate bugs. They're worried about their pets. They're worried about their children. They don't want to handle poison on their own. They'd rather pay a professional to come in and do it, whether in their house or in their place of business.

So look for the painful situations people are in, and sell to them. Find things that people would rather not do or can't be bothered to do, and then take away their pain. **Solve their problems for them.** This is really good news for an entrepreneur who doesn't have a lot of money, because there are plenty of services out there that you can get started for next to nothing. Even if you don't have a lot of money, for a couple hundred dollars you can start a business where you do things like paint houses or shovel snow. Here in Kansas, we even have companies that put up Christmas lights in the winter. You can clean out people's garages, deliver their groceries, haul away their junk cars, you name it. **The sky's the limit, and you don't need a lot of skills.** You just need to be willing to do the kinds of things that most people don't want to do. I've often thought that if I was dead broke and on the street, this is exactly what I'd do. Oh, I wouldn't do the work myself; I'd hire other people to do that. But I *would* go around knocking on doors, and whatever the customers needed done, I'd convince them that they could trust me to do it. I'd sell myself and my company, and in no time at all, the money would be flowing in—because I would be doing things for people that they didn't want to do for themselves. **I'd be looking for painful situations, and then I'd be fixing those situations in exchange for money.**

There's no reason to be broke! With a little ingenuity, you could be making money in almost no time flat. This concept is absolutely ideal for someone who doesn't have a large grubstake to start out with. Instead of sitting there, wishing and hoping for something that could make you a lot of money quickly, do a little thinking, pick up, and go! **Unfortunately, I think that most people overlook the simplicity of a strategy like this because they're looking for the big payday.** The want to hit the lottery, so to speak, with something that can bring them millions, so they're overlooking something that can bring them thousands in the meantime. They'll struggle to pay their mortgage, they'll be on the verge of bankruptcy, they can't make their car payment—because instead of thinking about what they could do to make just a few hundred bucks, they sit around wishing they had a way to make millions!

Start by making *some* money, and then build from there. That's the better way to look at it. If you're desperate, if you're broke, get out there and start making *some* money before you worry about making millions. This is a good way of doing that.

Again, the three proven ways to make money are to do something nobody wants to do; to do things others can't be bothered to do or would rather not do; and to do something you're great at that others are terrible at. Now, I'm talking about making money here, but I think that you see this philosophy in action elsewhere, too. Consider professional athletes, people who play sports for a living and get paid to do it. Most people just see the end result, and think "Oh, well, they're born with that talent." And it may be that they have some raw talent; but generally speaking, they became a professional athlete because they're dedicated to their craft. They're willing to do what it takes. They're willing to do something that nobody else is willing to do, which is to train for six or eight hours a day, or more, consistently. When they were younger and trying to make it in the sports business, they became, at some point, dedicated to the concept that they were going to be the best at their sport. They were committed to that.

Somebody who exercises may be gearing up for a marathon, or maybe they're just a health addict and they want to be healthy, or maybe they're committed to losing weight, or they need to get in shape just so they're around to see their kids graduate from high school. Whatever the motivating factor is, they've decided that they're going to exercise on a regular basis, and they're going to commit to, say, running every morning. I have friends tell me or write on Facebook about how many miles they ran this morning. **That's not something that most people would look at as being fun; it's something that most people don't want to do, and yet these people *are* doing it, because they want the end results that come with being in shape.**

Chris Lakey has a friend who's good at a wide variety of things, and he surprises Chris occasionally. The first time Chris saw him play electric guitar, his wife told Chris about how **he was really good at being determined to do something and then learning how to do whatever it was.** He happened to want to play guitar, and so he committed himself to practicing all the time and became good at it. He has the kind of personality where if he wants to do something, he does it right and he excels at it. He doesn't accept mediocrity in anything he commits to.

That's just another example of what I'm talking about here. This guy is doing something that other people don't want to be bothered to do, or would rather not do. **I think it comes down to being dedicated to the end goal, whatever that end goal is.** A lot of people dabble in things. For example, about 10 years ago as of this writing, Chris decided it would be fun to play around on the stock market. Oh, at the time he had his regular retirement account and similar things that were managed for him, and he never really had to pay any attention to them. He just knew they were out there, doing what they were supposed to. But he wanted to dabble in the stock market. So he opened an account at a brokerage, put a few thousand dollars in it, and played around. He wasn't dedicated to it; he didn't study the market well. He just bought stock in companies he was interested in, watched them for a while, then sold them.

One thing Chris looked for was IPOs, Initial Public Offerings. Back in those days, pretty much any Internet stock would blow up and go huge within minutes of going public, so he would play around with that a little bit. He lost a little money and made a little, and in the end, he pretty much just let the account dry up. He never made much money and never lost much, but he wasn't committed to it, so he didn't do it well. **I think a lot of people are that way with a lot of things. It's sort of like gambling.** They throw some money on the table and play a few hands, but they're never committed to winning as much as they can.

People do that in business, too. They might get involved in a network marketing opportunity and try that for a few weeks, then get bored and try something else. They've got all kinds of things working all the time—or not working, as the case may be—**but they're never committed to any single idea or to producing some specific result. They just dabble. They move on frequently and jump around to lots of different things.** The result would be similar if they were trying to master the art of sales copy, as I mentioned earlier. If you aren't committed fully to being a student of copywriting, and accomplishing the end goal of being a good copywriter, you might write a headline or a classified ad—you might dabble in it a little—but you would never achieve the results you might receive if you'd just stick to it.

Success requires a wholehearted dedication to the end goal that you're trying to achieve. That's what doing something nobody else wants to do means. No one else is interested in putting in the time. That's why true runners are rare; in fact, it's why people who are committed to doing any kind of daily exercise are rare. Most people would rather sit on their backsides and watch TV and eat potato chips, so being part of the tiny percentage of people who are committed to exercising regularly puts you above and beyond the average person.

In business, being dedicated to growing a thriving business, and doing everything you can to learn all you can about your marketplace and how to excel there, is something that most people are just not willing to see through. They quit too early, giving up before they reach success; all kinds of factors make them get in or out of a marketplace. **They're just not dedicated to the end goal.** That's one part of doing something that nobody else wants to do and going where nobody else wants to go: it's just being committed enough to see the end result happen.

Number three—doing something you're great at that others are terrible at—is really what carving out a niche in your marketplace is all about. You can come into that marketplace and provide that service or product with ease. That creates a demand for whatever it is you're good at. You often see this with people who start out as amateurs at something; they're not doing whatever it is for business or for profit, at least at first. For many years, Chris Lakey just happened to be handy with computers—and he's usually the go-to guy if there's a computer issue in the family or among his friends. They know that he's a computer user, not really an expert. He's not a programmer, *per se*, but he's been around computers long enough to understand them, and he uses them every day.

Chris can generally help someone fix their computer or try to get it to do something it's not doing, so if they have a question, he's the person they ask. He says he's not great at it, but he's good enough at it where a lot of other people aren't. **That's created a gap in people's minds. They know they're bad at it, so that creates a situation where he can offer advice on that front. The same kind of thing happens in business.** If you're good at plumbing or electrical work or you're a good mechanic, there are many, many people who *aren't* good at those things. **Therefore, you can create a business for yourself where you profit by solving problems people can't solve on their own.**

The greater the gap between the number of people who can do something and the number of people who can't, the greater the profits. If you're in a marketplace where there are thousands of people who provide a certain service or product, well, the demand for that will be relatively steady—whatever that demand may be. If you've got 1,000 people who can provide a service on one hand, and you've got 100 people who can provide another service, the marketers in the marketplace with 100 practitioners can charge more because there are fewer people to do it. **So look for places where there's a gap. It can start with something you're great at; but I would also encourage you instead to become great at something where**

that gap already exists. Don't just think, "Well, I'm only good at these two things, so one of these two things has to be my business." That's not necessarily true! You can become great at something by becoming dedicated to the end goal of being good at it. **You can find a marketplace where such a gap exists, and *then* create the greatness within yourself to fill that gap.**

Again, there are all kinds of ways to make money that meet these three criteria: things like going door-to-door washing windows or doing some groundskeeping. Lawn mowing is something that few people like to do, for example. Chris recently had to replace his lawnmower; he went and paid less than $300 for a new one. Now, I don't really know a whole lot about lawnmowers and whether he got a really good one or just an okay one, but it looked like it would do the job. So for a few hundred bucks, you have a brand new lawnmower. You can buy a used one for less if you want to... and *viola*, you can have a mowing business. If you have a pickup truck, you can throw the lawnmower in the back and drive across town and hustle up business. Before Chris got this lawnmower, he was paying someone who had mowed for him for a number of years, on and off. This guy came out and spent an hour of his time and got paid $30. He's got accounts all over town. It's easy, and there are all kinds of things like that you can do.

I see people on the corner of streets offering to wash windows. You see this in big cities a lot—people hustling business wherever they can get it, trying to provide a service to people and making a little money. **The three things I've been talking about offer great jumping off points for finding something you can do to start making money right away.**

Just doing something nobody wants to do, doing things that other people can't be bothered to do or would rather not do themselves, or something you're great at that others are terrible at—that's all there is to it. **Things like that create gaps in the marketplace between the want-to's and the don't-want-to's or the cans and can'ts.**

You can fill that gap and make money. There are *plenty* of things you can do to make a little bit of money—things you can do just to get started in business, just to get some money coming in, just to help pay a car payment or a house payment or rent—or to make sure your electricity doesn't get cut off. **These principles also work if you're trying to grow your business. By filling gaps in the marketplace between what people need done but don't want to do themselves, you can make a lot of money—no matter what your specific business is.**

Why don't more people do this? Because they just can't get past this whole idea of a J-O-B. So when they think of making money, they think of going and getting a job... and that becomes the prison cell they live their whole lives in. If there are no jobs, they sit around and cry like babies. They can be grown adults, and yet inside, they're like helpless children without their parents... because the only way that they know how to make money is to go out and get a job. I pray that you will never be like that, and praise you for reading this book so you can learn how not to be!

CHAPTER FOUR

Business is a combination of:

- ✓ **Art:** We paint the canvas.
- ✓ **War:** Battle the forces!
- ✓ **Science:** Specific tested formulas.
- ✓ **Sport:** Play the game!
- ✓ **Spiritual:** Disciplined. Focused.

Business is a Combination of Art, War, Science, Sports, and the Spiritual

This way of looking at business is somewhat different from most people's. A lot of us just think about business as a way to make more money or pay our bills. But many years ago, I read a quote that talked about business being other things besides just making money, and I've added to that list. Nowadays, **I've got five different metaphors that help me better understand what business means to me. These are the metaphors that drive me. They help me deal with the difficulties I face.** They've helped me get past some of the problems that I've had to get past. They've helped me view business in a different light, and get more enjoyment out of it. These days, I see business as a combination of art, war, science, sports... and even the spiritual.

Let's work that from back to front, starting with the spiritual. **That's how I see my business, when I'm thinking correctly: as a spiritual thing. I don't just do it for money. Now, when I think of spiritual things, the first things that come to mind are self-discipline and routine.** My daily routine is very important to me. I get up early every morning at about five o'clock. I get myself a pot of coffee and immediately go to work. This morning, I rose at 5:20 and spent the first few hours of my morning the way that I try to spend the first few hours of every morning, seven days a week: **I write. I think. I strategize.** This morning I wrote 2,000 words; that's a good day for me. I do that kind of thing every morning, first thing. It's part of my discipline.

Consider the martial arts, most of which are very spiritual. Most martial arts training takes place in something called a dojo, which is more than just a place to practice your fighting skills. It's part of the whole tradition of discipline. Martial arts isn't about going out and kicking people's asses; it's a way of life. **You find meaning in the practice itself. For me, every day is like that: a disciplined endeavor where I'm trying to constantly improve.** I'm very, very focused. I think our businesses are reflections of us; if business is bad, look in the mirror and point. So it's a spiritual thing for me.

And then there's the sports aspect. **To me, business is also a game. It's fun; it's challenging.** Now, years ago I did a word study of the word "challenging." A challenge is something that's difficult, yet provides you joy or fulfillment in trying to solve it. It's not just a problem, at least not in the sense that most people think of a problem. A problem is like: "Oh, my God." A challenge is: "Oh my God!" **It's something to get excited about. It's something to work towards.** When I think of sports, I think of something that's very difficult—yet within that difficulty, there's a real satisfaction that comes from trying.

Business is also a science, in the sense that there are formulas involved, things that are interchangeable from one business to another. Something that works well in one business will usually work well in another. Chris Lakey and I were recently having a discussion about our new retail store. We've never been in the retail business, but we're involved with several other people who have been, and we're using proven models from other retail businesses that have nothing to do with our own store. **We're finding ways to incorporate some of the ideas that other businesses have used successfully. There's a science behind all this.** Not only are moneymaking ideas interchangeable, there are certain mathematical formulae that apply to business. You know what something costs you versus what it makes you. **Plus, you test things in small ways; and then, if the numbers pan out, you simply roll out and do more of what you tested, and you get more money pouring in.** That's another example of the scientific nature of business.

I also see business as a war. I see every day as a battle, some days more than others. Victor Hugo, the great French Revolutionist, once said, "Those who live are those who fight." I love the sound of that, and the image that it creates: **Those businesses that succeed are the businesses that *fight*.** They're the ones that refuse to quit! Years ago, I heard that success is simply outrunning failure, and I thought it was a cute little saying. And yet, now that I've been self-employed for 25 years, I know that this is true—because so many people just give up. **The only way you can *really* fail is to quit. As long as you haven't quit, you haven't failed.** And it *does* take a certain fighter mentality. You need to be the person who refuses to quit, the person who will not be beaten; they can be beat, but they can't be *beaten*. You can knock them down 20 times, and they'll get up 21 times.

You have to be like Paul Newman in that 1967 movie *Cool Hand Luke*. There's a scene where he's getting crushed by George Kennedy's character. Kennedy is three times bigger, he's three times stronger, and he's three times better at fighting than Paul Newman is. He keeps knocking Newman down... and Newman refuses to quit. He keeps getting up, to the point where Kennedy's character realizes that the only way to beat this man is to either beat him unconscious or kill him. Otherwise, Kennedy can only give up and let him live—and that's what he does. So Newman ultimately wins that fight, in my eyes; at least, he wins the respect of all the men around him. He's a fighter!

Business is tough, and you've got to be tougher. You've got to be harder than whatever comes at you. You've got to be stronger than all the problems you're going to face along the way. **And it *does* require the mindset of a warrior: somebody who refuses to be beaten, who is going to keep on struggling no matter what.** You can knock them down but you can't beat them. They're just going to keep coming at you. All great entrepreneurs have that fighting spirit inside of them.

Last but not least, the fifth metaphor is art. I see business as a very creative pursuit, one limited only by imagination. Therein lies the challenge, though, because a lot of people have lost their ability to be imaginative. **They've lost their ability to create.** They've got blinders on, so they can't see all the possibilities. Then too, so much in business is speculative! We don't know how it's going to go; we just have to believe it before we see it. **We're the ones who make it real, the ones who create it.** We're the ones who come up with all the bold, fresh, innovative, outside-the-box ideas that keep businesses alive. **Many times those ideas fail, but every once in a while they're accepted in the marketplace, and they**

bring in millions of dollars. That's part of the game; but that's also part of the art of it. That's also part of the challenge of it. That's the purpose of the war; that's the battle part of it, that's the sporting part of it.

Chris Lakey and I are working on a unique publishing idea right now. We've going to start with four different publications, but we have an idea for an endless number of similar ones. All in all, we have a goal of selling anywhere from 10-30 million books! Now, are the odds against us? You better believe they are. Come on—10-30 million books! **The odds are very much against us, and yet we've got a solid plan; it's creative, we're thinking outside of the box, we're not limited by our imaginations, we're willing to fight with a gale force. It's something that we're dedicated and passionate about. And again, it may fail miserably. That's part of the challenge of it all.**

Look, if it was easy, everybody would be doing it. But if it *was* easy, where would the challenge be? It's only in facing the uncertainties, in going against the odds and trying to do everything possible to turn it around, that you find the joy. That's where the hero's journey is; it's a concept that shows up in all kinds of great stories, where one person fights against a much larger force, where they endure the battle and come out victorious in the end. That story has shown up again and again for thousands of years, in spoken tradition and stories and fables, and more lately in books and television and movies.

You've got to strive for more than the money! If you're in business for the money alone, then you're never going to get a sense of joy and fulfillment out of it, and chances are

you're never even going to succeed at it. Because again, you're in it for the wrong reasons. So let these metaphors drive you; let them help you develop a bigger vision of what business is. And certainly, it's an outlet for all your ambition: just trying to see how high you can go, what you're capable of. **How high is high for you?** It's also a part of an extension of who you are, in the sense that it's an expression of you—who you are and what you're all about. These are things that will help carry you through the hard times and give you so much more joy and fulfillment in the end.

When I think of art I often think of painting, and the canvas as it relates to business. An artist might look at a blank canvas and ask himself: "What do I want this to be?" Well, it could be anything! Maybe you could paint a picture of somebody; maybe you can paint a landscape, or an animal. It could be anything you want it to be... within your abilities as an artist, obviously. A blank canvas is an open invitation to be creative.

As it relates to business, I think of the possibilities for a project to take on many different shapes or forms. **One of the reasons I love being in the information marketing business is that information products can be whatever we want them to be.** Much like an artist, we can create the end product that we want, whatever that may be. As information marketers, we start with an idea for a product or a service of some kind, and we create the offer. We create the sales letter that will sell it, and as we're creating that, it's sort of like an artist putting their impressions on the canvas.

We ask ourselves: "What is this?" And really the answer to

that is: "Whatever we want it to be!" **When we look at creating an offer, we know our marketplace, and so we create an offer that attempts to give the people in our marketplace exactly what they want.** Usually, what that ends up meaning is that we have a lot of liberty regarding exactly what our product is going to be. **It could take a variety of shapes or sizes. That's what makes business a form of art:** your offer is the blank piece of canvas you're getting ready to paint on; at the beginning, it can take any form, depending on your imagination. **All you really do is start by considering the framework—the benefit you provide to your marketplace. Then you build on it.**

Business is also like war, in that you're battling other forces that want you to fail. There's always an enemy, someone you're fighting against. One of the enemies of business success in general is what we call the Beast of Negativity. In fact, many years ago we created a product called "No Negativity." It actually had an illustration featuring a gentleman in a suit holding up a big sword and slaying the Beast of Negativity. In a sense, you're battling the forces of evil in your business: all the negative junk, all the distractions, all the things that can keep you from accomplishing your end goal of serving your marketplace and making a profit for yourself and your business. **You have to constantly strive against those negative forces.**

One of the ways you do that is by being alert and aware and prepared for battle. Let's say you're a lazy general. Your troops are sitting around laughing and playing cards; they're all drunk, because they've been partying it up. If an enemy attacks you, your troops get slaughtered, because no one is prepared for battle. That's your fault, as their leader. The same thing can happen in business. **If you're not prepared for battle, you get complacent—you get lazy, distracted, slack... and when the enemy attacks, you're not prepared to fight back.**

So stay positive, constantly aware that there are all kinds of people out there who will tell you that you *can't* do something. It's easy for people to be skeptics or critics, especially when it comes to business. People will ask you: "Why are you making a crazy decision like that? Don't follow your heart, use your *head*. Don't launch a business. Go back to school and get a degree! Succeed the normal way." As if there *is* such a thing. So you have to be aware that there are forces out there that are against you succeeding, and they won't hesitate to attack you; and if you're not prepared for that, you can easily succumb. Because you know what? **All business is risky.** It doesn't matter who the entrepreneur is or what the situation is: most businesses fail. **But if you know that going in, you can prepare yourself to do battle against the people and things out there that tell you that you can't or shouldn't do it. Battling those forces is important.**

At M.O.R.E., Inc., we talk a lot about math and psychology and the formulas for success. **That's because business really is a lot like a scientific equation. At its root, it's about profits and losses. It's a lot more complex than that, sure; but at its most basic, business is about summing up and calculating the risks you want to take, and choosing your battles as they relate to that.** So you follow the formulas in your model, and those formulas will lead you to income; and it's that income, based against your costs and your advertising and your overhead, that will determine your profitability. In the end, you look at the numbers and determine whether you've made a profit; and if you haven't, you go back to the drawing board and try another. **You don't quit; you just try a new way to achieve a different result.** That's what science is all about. Accountants lie; math doesn't. Two plus two is always four. Either you're making a profit or you're not.

Business is also like sports. When Chris Lakey was in junior high, he had a friend who was always trying to get him to take karate classes with him. Back then, Chris thought karate was just about learning how to beat people up. It was an aggressive, offensive sport. You learn karate so that you can chop at people and kick them, right? Well, I've never taken any classes, but as I understand it, karate isn't intended to be merely offensive; it's a defensive art as well. It's based on centering yourself and focusing. There's a lot more to martial arts than the offensive practices of kicking and chopping and doing all the things you see in Bruce Lee movies.

That's how business relates to sports. **It's about playing the game and trying to master it, trying to be the best you can—and, of course, trying to win!** It's a many-faceted thing. To a baseball player, it's not just about hitting the ball, and it's not just about pitching. **It's about the conditioning that goes into the sport;** it's about getting ready for game day, not just the moment the ball comes across the plate and you have to choose whether to swing or stand by and hope it's a ball. **It's all the other things that go into the preparations for playing the game. And you want to play it to win.**

As far as spirituality goes: we're spiritual beings, beings with souls, and that means we tend to think about things from that aspect. **Discipline and focus and, certainly, spirituality take different forms for different people; but I think that the spiritual element to life translates to business as well—especially if you meditate, pray, focus, or whatever form that takes for you.** In business that usually just mean focus; but it can also mean taking some time to relax and meditate about your business. You can think about how you're serving your customers, or about any number of things relating to your business. It's an aspect of life—and so I think that means that it has to be an aspect of business. **This spiritual aspect of business just comes along with being spiritual beings with souls.** There are very few true atheists or agnostics; most people believe in some kind of religious experience, and whatever shape that takes for you, it can come out in the way you think about your business.

Consider top entrepreneurs, the ones who make it in the biggest kind of way. The danger is to somehow think that those people are special, that they have something that you don't. That's not true. **For the most part, they're normal people; they just see business differently than most people see it.** These are the five metaphors that I've came up with to interpret the business experience... but maybe for those people, there are other metaphors. Maybe some see business is a lifestyle, for example. I've certainly thought about that. Of course, metaphor are mutable: you can take one thing and find many different meanings, associations and connections for it. **The point is, this process helps you to deepen your understanding of things; it gives you a different perspective, a different way**

of looking at something. I'm convinced that all successful entrepreneurs think of business as so much more than just making money—whether they do consciously or not.

This is one thing that sets them apart from employees, I think. **Most people who have what I call the "employee mindset" just think about money. That's what they work for, and that's about it.** While I'm sure there are some employees who don't work only for the money, too often, people see work as just a way of paying the bills... something they do to bring in money so they can have their regular life. All they worry about is making enough money for the things they enjoy, that they're passionate about.

Entrepreneurs are exactly the opposite. The work itself is something special. Their vocation is their vacation. Their work is their hobby. Their work is their *passion*. It's something they truly put themselves into wholeheartedly. Other people see these entrepreneurial people devoting large chunks of their life to work, and they think that somehow, there's something wrong with those people—but there's nothing wrong with them at all. **Their work is an extension of themselves.** Their work is all of these things I've talked about in this chapter, and more.

We used to have a seminar center, this huge metal building, with all these motivational banners hanging up on the wall to liven it up little bit. One of those banners said: "Concepts first, details last." In a sense, a metaphor is a concept: an overall, overarching idea. **I think part of the game of business, part of the art of it, part of the scientific nature of it, is thinking about it in a generalized, conceptual way.**

You start with a goal—like this goal we've set with our good friend Russ von Hoelscher, where we plan to sell anywhere from 10-30 million books. That's kind of a scientific equation, where we begin with the end in mind. Our goal is to sell millions of books. We've got some general ideas of how we're going to do it, how we're going to enter the marketplace in a different way; there are some unique things we're going to try. But at the moment, it's just spark of an idea, a hazy, conceptual kind of idea. We're beginning with the end goal in mind, and we're trying to see how far we can go. **We're thinking very clearly about the people who are going to buy our books. That's where all of this really does start, because without the marketplace, you have no business at all.**

And let me touch, again, on your enemies here. **Man, when comes to business, there are all kinds of enemies out there—including your friends and family, who are often the naysayers of your life.** These are the people who are telling you all the reasons why you're an idiot to think you're ever going to accomplish anything significant. They can be worse than your competitors, the people who are trying to steal away the same customers you're trying to attract. Add in the various market forces, which are constantly changing the dynamics of the marketplace, and there is just so much opposition!

As for the spiritual aspects: again, I'm not talking about religion, necessarily... although in a way I do see business as my religion (and I don't mean that sacrilegiously). **From the spiritual perspective, it's about giving, serving, trying to add value. Those are concepts that I think of as spiritual.** There's a spiritual concept that goes, "As within, so without." It all starts with making the invisible visible: with taking these invisible ideas and trying to manifest them as reality. This is something that creates jobs, something that creates money; again, it goes back to the old concept that you've got to believe it before you see it. That's a very spiritual concept. **It's got to be real inside of you before you can manifest it in the marketplace. It requires a lot of faith and belief.**

Think about all this; ponder the way that business is, truly, a combination of the concepts I've laid out in this principle. There are just three proven ways to make money. That's conceptual in nature, too. **Develop your awareness of different businesses that are out there doing well, and consider what's behind those businesses.** What are the dynamics that created them in the first place, and are making them successful today? **Because nothing happens by accident in the business world.** Oh, maybe these people got lucky by accident, because they stumbled onto the right set of ingredients, and now all of sudden they're making big money. But in the bright light of the day, when you hold it under the magnifying glass, you'll find that the business is succeeding for specific reasons. **Once you know those reasons, then you have the ability to perhaps interchange some of their main ideas into your business, and cash-in on them with unique twists of your own.**

You absolutely must think of business as so much more than just making money. Now, I realize that the only reason some of you are reading this is that you think you have to, because you want to make more money. **But a true business is something much more than just that; and if you focus on**

these other things, the irony is that you'll be more likely to succeed. That's a paradox: by dedicating and committing yourself to your business in all these ways, by putting your entire self into your business—that's a spiritual concept, by the way—you give it everything that you possibly have. **Lay it all on the line; put every ounce of your entire being into something. Assuming you stay very focused on the marketplace, the money will follow.**

CHAPTER FIVE

The Relationship Model:

1. Think customers — not sales.
2. Build relationships.
3. Spend money consistently to communicate with your customers.
4. Somehow we must convince them that...
   - *We care.*
   - *We want to help.*
   - *We want to serve.*
   - *And do <u>more</u> for them than any competitor.*

The Relationship Model

In case you haven't noticed it yet, we're all in the relationship business. That's an over-generalization, of course, perhaps even an over-simplification; but it's still true at a very basic level. Your customers have more choices than ever before about where they can spend their money. They're more picky than they've ever been. **They're harder to reach and harder to communicate with and harder to build relationships with.** It's harder than ever to get them to come back again and again—and yet it's more important than ever to do so.

Anybody who tells you there's a simple, easy way to create and maintain relationships with your customers is lying to you. Yes, there are some simple formulas and principles that you can use to guide you; and yet, actually accomplishing this is very difficult. Don't let anybody tell you otherwise. **But there's a wonderful reward for the work: a payoff in profits. All the profits that you want to make come from reselling to your existing customers.** To do that, you've got to build solid relationships with them.

That doesn't mean that you have to spend quality time with each and every one. Our parent company has thousands of customers; and in my opinion, we do a really good job of building and maintaining relationships with our customers. **Do we have some customers who don't like us? Yes, we do. We**

try, but it's impossible to keep every customer happy. We have customers who don't like us, we have angry customers, and occasionally we have problems that we have to work through with our customers. **But we also have thousands of customers who do business with us again and again.** That's the simple secret for profitability, and it can make you very, very wealthy—which is why it's worth going through all the headaches and hassles, the time and the work, required to do all these things.

My relationship model consists of four principles that I call the Four Pillars. Think of a chair with four different legs; each of these principals is like one of those legs. If you get all four of them right, you have a very solid foundation to rest on. **Here's the FIRST: think about customers, *not* just sales.** Plenty of salespeople are good at bringing in the customers initially, but somebody can't really be considered a customer until they come back three or four times. **Your job is to get people to come back. Your business plan should be a long-term one, so you've *got* to get them back.**

I've already mentioned the restaurant model in several of these principles. Think about your favorite restaurant, one that you've gone to for years. Chances are, they've done a good job of building a relationship with you. **They make you feel good. They know what you like, and they know what you don't like.** If they're a really popular restaurant, then they're always filled, so you know they're doing the same with other people: they're building bonds with them. **That's really your goal here. You've got to think about customers in the long term. Your job is to get them back repeatedly, and you do that by continuing to give them what they want.** If your business is a restaurant, it's food. Even if you don't have a restaurant, your job is to continue to give customers whatever they've come to you for in the first place—or at least, similar types of things.

NUMBER TWO, you've got to build those relationships. This doesn't happen by accident. One of the ways we've gone about building relationships and friendships with our customers is by expressing all of our commonalities with them. **We tell them our story to illustrate this point.** We share it over and over again—to the point where some of our customers have heard it a million times and get sick and tired of it. And the truth is, I'm sick and tired of telling it over and over again! If I never had to tell our story again—how we began, and all the things we have in common with our clients—it would be too soon! But I do it for a reason. First of all, I do it for the customers who haven't heard it yet, or have forgotten it. Never assume everyone will remember. **When you've got a good story that links you to the people you sell to repeatedly, you've *got* to tell that story over and over.** Just because you're tired of telling it doesn't mean your customers are tired of hearing it.

The THIRD of our Four Pillars is simply this: we constantly stay in touch with people. You've got to spend money consistently to communicate with your customers, and I'm not just talking about email here. Email is *one* way to stay in touch with your customers, sure, and now we have social media like Facebook and Twitter. **However you approach them and maintain contact, segment out your best customers from the rest, and don't be afraid to spend extra money on them, doing things that make an impact with them over a period of**

time. And yes, it's easier said than done.

One of the things we do with our customers is constantly bombard them with mail. We're always making new and different offers. Look, your customers are buying from other people who sell things similar to the things you sell. You have to assume that your most rabid customers *are* doing that, and there's plenty of indirect competition also—that is, other places they can spend money that don't sell the exact same kinds of things you do. **With all the competition out there, you can't really build a relationship if you never spend any real time with people.** It does take work.

And last but not least, the **FOURTH Pillar: You have to constantly look for ways to show people you care about them, that you're there to *serve* them.** Prove that you're trying to do more for them than any of your competitors. Just watch what other companies are doing; pay especially close attention to companies that are doing a great job of serving their customers. **Good customer service can work wonders, and that service attitude will bond people to you.** It never ceases to amaze me how somebody can spend a fortune building a really great company—and then put people with bad attitudes behind the counters. But it happens constantly. The people who are face-to-face with the customers, or on the phone with the customers, *must* be pleasant people with good attitudes who understand the importance of service. Anything else is just crazy! **Good customer service is a form of marketing. It's a marketing expense.** Marketing, of course, is all the things you do to acquire customers and get them to come back... and certainly that's what good customer service does for you.

Remember, we're all in the relationship business. **We're all trying to do things that set us apart from the competition. First and foremost, the attractor factor: there's got to be something different about what you're doing.** The relationship factor keeps them coming back, because they *do* have a lot of choices about where they could be spending their money. **You want them to choose you, always; a relationship encourages that, and it's really what separates a good business from a bad one.**

Of course, we're not talking about Wal-Mart or any of the big national retailers here. In that circumstance, the person who owns or runs the company isn't the face of the company. **But with a small business, the ability to build long-term relationships with your clients is crucial, since it's responsible for the ultimate success or failure of your business.** So, as you consider the model for your business, you've got to include this relationship factor. Admittedly, this can be hard to quantify, because what *is* a relationship? What does it mean? What does it look like?

Well, since your goal in business is to make a profit and serve your customers so that they continue to do business with you, you have to focus more on who they are, and not so much on just making a sale. Just making the sale and blowing off the customer works only if you're a monopoly or in the fad business—that is, if you're selling something that's here today and gone tomorrow and you're trying to make a quick buck. There's not necessarily anything wrong with that; it's just not a good, sustainable business model. It's fine if you're selling a fad item like the Snuggy. The Snuggy used to be all over the commercials on TV. I know they still sell them—you can see them in the stores—but there was a short while there where it was talked about constantly, and the commercial was running all the time.

With those kinds of products, who cares about relationships? The goal is to get the public to become aware of the fad item, and to get them to want to purchase one for themselves. You want millions and millions of people to buy, and there's no residual business there, no back-end. You get a customer, you make a sale, and you move on. That's a kind of inventor's market. **They invent these kinds of products, sell them, and they move on to other things, and there's no relationship with the client at all.**

That's not the way that most businesses should operate, and yet you often see that the focus is entirely on making the sale today, and not at all on building a relationship with the client. In those instances, you have a store that does nothing to capture contact information; they do nothing to make you feel welcome, to find out who you are or what you're interested in or what you're looking for. They want you to buy something while you're there, and they hope you see an ad sometime in the future and come back later—but they're not going to try to do anything to build that relationship.

So what does a good relationship look like? What do you need to do in order to build relationships? Well, let's forget about business for a minute. **If you have a friend, the way you build a relationship is not to ignore them! You want to show them that you care.** You do that by calling them on the phone, by dropping by where they work or live, and making your presence known. You communicate with them on a regular basis, you go out to dinner, you go out and go watch a movie. You hang out. **There's a two-way communication in play: you talk to them and they talk to you, and the relationship grows.** Eventually, it may move from casual friendship to some sort of a deeper friendship. You hang out with them all the time, you can finish each other's sentences, you know all about them and what they're interested in. If there was a dating game for buddies, you would be able to go on it and win, because you know everything about your bud!

That relationship solidifies as you continue to hang out together, as you continue to talk and build that relationship. It works similarly in the business arena, though it can take on different shapes and forms; but generally speaking, you don't build a relationship by ignoring a customer. **You build a relationship by talking to them, by spending time and money communicating with them.** This is why you see a lot of businesses circulate newsletters, whether electronically or in print (which used to be the only option). **Whatever the method, it means spending time and money (and time *is* money) to communicate with your customers.** The newsletter is just one way that businesses do that. You tell them what's going on in your store, and you make them a special offer or two. Ideally, this isn't just for the purpose of making a sale; **when done well, it's an altruistic communication with a friend, showing them that you want something more than just the dollar in their wallet.**

Of course, your ultimate goal in business is to make a profit; so there's no hiding that you're there to be in

business. But you can do that by serving them, by making them believe that they're the most important client in the store. It's like a restaurant where you've gone many times: they know just what you like. When you come in, they remember the table where you like to sit, and they know that this or that is your favorite dish; you don't even have to order it, because they already *know*. Well, you're not their only important client; it's part of their business practice that they know a lot about their clients. That's why they make an effort to remember your favorite drink. **They make you feel special,** even though you may not be that special to them. They're really there to get you to order more and to buy another drink, so they get a bigger tip.

And so even though you give the *appearance* that each customer is ultimately the most important client you have, you do that to everybody. Really, you don't play favorites; you like all your customers, and you treat them all with respect, and you learn as much as you can about all of them because you want to build those relationships. They have to realize and believe that you care about them (which is true), that you want to help them, that you're there to serve them, that you want to do more for them than any competitor they'll ever encounter. If they make the mistake of visiting one of your competitor's stores, they're going get such a bad taste in their mouth from that experience, in comparison with their experience with you, that they'll never go back.

That close relationship allows you an entry into their world, giving you the ability to make your presentation to them. If you have someone who's just trying to sell you something and you know they're *just* out to get your money, you tend to tune them out. You see what they're after, and you don't want to give it to them. **But if you have a relationship with somebody and they're making a suggestion to you, that comes across differently.** If a friend of yours says, "Hey, I recommend you go and see this movie!" that comes across a lot differently than if a theater sends you an ad in the mail saying the same thing. You know that they want you to watch the movie because they want your $10 for the ticket, not to mention all the money you'll pay on popcorn and drinks.

There's a different feel to a relationship than there is to a plain client/business interaction. As weird as it may sound, if you can get your customers to feel like they're in a relationship with you, they're less likely to cheat on you with other businesses. So put the relationship model into play, and your customers will be more loyal, they'll spend more money with you, they'll feel better doing business with you; **and in the end, if you serve them right and sincerely, your business will see an increase in sales and profitability because of it.**

Chapter Six

Stories Sell!

You must create powerful stories that captivate your prospects and customers. These are stories about you, your company, or your products or services.

Choose your stories carefully. They must sound real. They have to be believable and emotional. *There should be some drama!* Some special secret — or a perceived benefit or promise to the reader.

Stories help you make the sale when nothing else will.

Stories Sell!

You have to create powerful stories to captivate your prospects and customers. **These stories about you, your company, your products and your services will do a great job of selling people on the things you want to sell. But choose your stories carefully: they must sound real, they must sound believable, and they must be emotional.** There should be some drama there: some special secret or perceived benefit or promise to the reader. Stories will help you make sales where nothing else will. **They go underneath the radar of people's sales resistance.** Whenever you're pitching somebody on something, they're trying to resist your sales message—whether it's conscious or unconscious on their part. Many times it's unconscious. In any case, they know you're trying to get them to give up their money, and they're trying to hang on to it. The shield is up! **But a story lowers people's guards.** Everybody loves to hear a story, so you're able to slip your message in under the shield when you tell them one—or over the wall of their skepticism and sales resistance, if you will.

People remember stories. **You can use stories to make the prospect understand certain things that you want them to understand, and you can use them to make effective comparisons between what you're selling and other things.** I'll give you some examples in a moment, but remember this: never compare apples to apples. **Always compare apples to**

oranges. In other words, compare what you're selling with something far more valuable; or if it's a complicated thing, compare it to something that they already understand.

Stories, analogies, metaphors: all are ways to get people involved and interested. If you're telling stories about yourself, it helps to build bonds between you and the prospect. One of the reasons people have so much sales resistance is that they're skeptical. **If you're telling stories about yourself that they can relate to, then you're going to win their hearts; and when you do that, you'll eventually win their business, too.** Stories are very emotional things... but then, that's what we sell to: people's emotions.

In creating your stories, think them through very carefully. **Develop them over a period of time; practice telling stories to other people, and try to get good at it.** We all know people in our lives who are really good at telling stories. Our good friend, Russ von Hoelscher, is a great story teller. Recently, we were in Dallas for a big seminar. All the speakers were there, sitting around the table, and we got Russ to tell some of his favorite stories. Some of these are stories I've heard maybe 20 times; but some of the speakers hadn't heard them, and even the ones who had all wanted to hear Russ tell them again. That's because Ross is a great storyteller!

Some people are naturals, **but this is a skill you can learn;** you can get better at it. And you should strive to do so, because stories can make you a lot of money. I've said it before and I'll say it again: our story, which is part of our USP, has made us millions of dollars. **It's been largely responsible for our fortune, because it's a rags-to-riches story that has all the**

elements in it to bond us to the people we sell to. Our story is really *their* story, too. Let me re-emphasize that it's commonality that builds friendships... and people like to do business with people whom they perceive as friends.

So our story about all the years that we spent searching for ways to make money, and how we kept getting ripped off and lied to—that's their story! Like we did, they're sending away for all kinds of things that mostly don't work. They're frustrated and confused, just like we were for years. Not that we've got it all figured out yet; to this day, we still get ripped off and lied to sometimes. But we've broken through that, in large part, and figured things out. **Our story is their story; that's one example of the power of stories, and how they build bonds with people.**

And again, you can compare what you're doing with other things, but not precisely the same types of things. Like I said earlier, never compare apples to apples. Here is an example of comparing apples to oranges. Years ago we had some unique websites; in fact, we were one of the very first developers of business e-books when they first came out. For the marketer, the appeal to e-books is that there's no product to be shipped; it's sent electronically, and that's also how the money is delivered. **In order to explain these websites, we called them "ATM websites."** We told people that they were the next best thing to having their own ATM money machine. And we even went down to our local bank and took a picture of their ATM machine (we put it on page five of our sales letter). **By comparing this new process with an ATM machine, we added a certain sexiness to it, and it did make a difference.**

We've also sold many different beta tester positions over the years. In order to help people understand what beta testers are all about, we talked about how software companies use beta testers to help them get all the bugs out of their software before it's ready to enter the general marketplace. Everything that's software related has to be beta-tested. Explaining to people how that's done on a day-in, day-out basis in the software industry helped them understand things a bit more clearly. **That's one of the reasons why you tell stories: they help people understand and remember things.**

When we started selling eBay back in 2002-2003, Vice President Dick Chaney had recently said some interesting things about eBay. So we used his picture and his story to sell our presence there. **It stuck in people's minds; it added credibility to what we were doing, and they remembered it.** When we started selling teleseminars (which you can't really do effectively anymore), we compared them to real seminars. We told people about all the things that you'd have to go through if you went to a real seminar, and how they could avoid doing all that just by sitting in their favorite easy chair and picking up the phone. **Stories like these make things more clear, and they add value.**

We have a new program out there called the Direct Pay System that I've mentioned once or twice before. When we're selling this program, we tell our story about how people are getting ripped off, they're getting lied to, they're not getting the money that they deserve. And again, we're getting people to relate to us by telling them these things. They're familiar with being treated this way. **This lowers their sales resistance; the**

stories help them see what we're offering to give them, and helps them want what we're selling even more.

One more example. We've got a new program we've recently started promoting as of this writing, and it's based on a powerful story that Russ von Hoelscher told me recently in Dallas. Once upon a time, he was at a seminar on self-publishing, as a teacher—a seminar people paid thousands of dollars to attend. After he was done presenting, a lady came up to him and handed Russ a book. She said, "Russ, I loved your presentation. I wanted you to see my book, and hear what you think about it." It was a certain type of novelty book; Russ looked at it and said, "Ma'am, I've seen things like this before. Don't get your hopes up too high. The bookstores won't take you, but you can probably get it in some gift stores." And she said, "Russ, you don't understand. I've already sold a million and a half of these books."

That's a great story! Russ tells it a million times better than me, of course, and he tells it with greater detail, but it's a great story, whoever tells it! **That story captivated me, and we've been telling that story during our latest promotion.** That story is going to be central to our sales message, because it resonates with people. It adds a level of credibility and believability, which is essential in the selling process, and it's something people easily remember. There are many directions you can take storytelling—a lot of different things you can do with it.

Stories are an effective tool in the selling process, and they transcend the media. You can use verbal storytelling, if you're platform selling at a conference. You can tell stories on an audio CD, if you're using recorded audio. You can tell a story in print, on paper or online. You can convey a story any number of ways; **storytelling isn't dependent on you using a certain type of media to convey your message.**

Your stories can be either true or fictional, depending on the scenario. **And of course, you don't want to tell a story that you purport to be true that is, in fact, made up.** Furthermore, a story can be yours or someone else's. The point is, a good story also transcends the selling process, in the sense that people don't hear or process a story the same way they process a sales presentation. If you're trying to sell something to someone and you throw in a story in the middle of it, the mind stops processing what it's hearing as a sales presentation and goes into story-listening mode. **Incorporating stories therefore helps people's brains process your presentation on the subconscious level, in a much more positive way (for you), as opposed to you just spending an hour trying to convince them to buy your product.** That's why you need to incorporate stories into your pitches.

The way you tell your story is also going to go a long way toward the success or failure of your endeavor. Obviously you need to know it by heart, but you also have to present it effectively. Let's say your story is typically a 30-minute presentation. But even if it takes 30 minutes to tell your story in full detail, maybe your best story is actually only a 10-minute story... so you want to cut out 20 minutes. Well, which 20 minutes do you cut out? **The remain 10 minutes is the part that you commit to memory, so that it becomes a story that you could tell in your sleep.** You know what parts you want to emphasize. You know what parts you *don't* want to emphasize.

You want to put your story in the best light, and so your story becomes a condensed version of the real story of you. The real story includes, well, let's see, "I was born in this year, and this date's my birthday. When I left the hospital, my mom dropped me on my head. I recovered from that okay. Then I went on to preschool. After preschool, I went to kindergarten, and then I finally made it to first grade."

Your story is a long, drawn-out affair, and there are parts that are inconsequential to what you're trying to accomplish in selling your products or services. **That's why you've got to condense it down to the most important parts... at least from your listener's perspective.** Earlier, I gave you a very condensed version of my life, which related directly to the marketplace I'm trying to reach. The larger story, which I also tell over and over again to build relationships with my customers, is all about my life and business and my struggle to find a way to make money. It culminates with my success in finally finding something that worked, and my mission to share that with other people. **There's much more to it than that, but most parts aren't important to my listeners.**

Your real, true story is not you sitting down and telling everybody when and where you were born and the whole minutiae—all the boring details no one cares about. **Your story becomes that small part of it that relates to what you're trying to convey to your prospects.** If you're selling a health product because it helped you lose weight and be more fit and have six-pack abs, or something along those lines, then your story isn't so much about how and where you grew up. It's that you lived a miserable life and you struggled with your weight and people made fun of you all the time, until you discovered XYZ product, or XYZ fitness regimen. Now all the ladies stare at you and you like going to the pool with your shirt off. That relates directly to what you're trying to sell, so that becomes your true story.

With a fake story, you're really talking about an illustration; a parable if you will. You're trying to make a point. You're not trying to lie to people; you have to be clear about that. Jesus told such stories, such parables, to convey messages to his disciples and followers. They weren't necessarily true stories, but they did effectively illustrate the points that he was trying to make. You could do the same to present a point that *you're* trying to make. Your story could be about two guys: one's doing one thing, the other some other thing, and both of them are traveling down similar roads; but one discovers this wonderful item, and the other keeps on going. The one that discovered this wonderful thing, which is related to what you're selling, lived a happier, more fulfilled life than Person B, who just kept doing what he was doing. **That's an example of a story that's not true, but still illustrates the point you're trying to make. Again, the point is not to lie to people.** You have to tell them that this is a fictitious story, a fable for teaching purposes.

You can also tell quick true stories about your experiences without getting to your core story. Maybe you're just telling a story about something that happened to you the other day. This isn't your main life story, it's something you're using to convey your message to them or to get them to understand who you are. **It's just a story to break the ice or help people identify with**

you—to help them understand who you are and what you're all about. One of these could come early in the process of selling. If you're on an audio recording, it could be an icebreaker: "Something funny happened to me the other day..." It could be a story to illustrate a point that you're trying to make a bit later in your sales presentation. You've already told them who you are; you've explained your story. **But then, a little bit later in the process, you're telling them something that happened to you recently, or some kind of other story, in order to press home the point you're trying to make at that moment in your selling process.**

Telling someone else's story usually involves a true story, too. It's a story you've heard from someone—possibly a friend or acquaintance who experienced this or that. Or you overheard someone tell it, or you read an article about somebody who did something. These are all along the lines of what I was talking about a little bit ago, when I discussed the eBay product that we created years ago. We used quotes from the Vice President and from other people of authority. **Those aren't necessarily long, drawn-out stories, but they become micro-stories about their experiences with something.** In that case, it was what the Vice President thought about eBay as a marketplace. It wasn't this long, drawn out story; it was just a paragraph. But it effectively illustrated the point we were trying to make. In that case, we were trying to show people that eBay really was a big deal, and worth their time to look at and explore. Using a quote from Dick Cheney was a good way to get people to realize that a lot of people are talking about this.

So you can use other people's stories and examples, as

long as you cite the source. If it's not an original thought, just be sure to say, "I heard this story from my good friend, so and so," or "This story came from *Newsweek*... Last week, I was reading about this, and here's what I learned from that, and here's why this applies to you." **Without recreating the entire story, you can read a paragraph or two and cite them, and you're fine doing so.**

Stories are so important, and they can be devastatingly effective. Whether they're true or fables, whether they're your own stories or someone else's, there are all kind of ways to incorporate them in your selling process. Like I said at the beginning of this chapter, there's something in the brain that switches gears when you go from selling to storytelling. **People receive and process stories differently; they're much more receptive to what you're telling them in story format, and tend to believe what's told to them—whereas if you're just selling, people are automatically skeptical.** And certainly, if you're telling a true story, that's to your benefit... though even when you're telling a story about a fake situation, people's brains switch gears. It comes across differently. **So use stories, and they will help you make the sale even when other things aren't working like they should.**

In the next chapter, **I'm going to tell you one of the most powerful stories I've ever heard in my life.** So hang on, because it illustrates our next principle.

Chapter Seven

Ruthless marketing has nothing to do with ripping people off. In fact, it's just the opposite.

It's all about extracting the largest amount of sales and profits from your targeted marketplace... And to do this — you must re-sell to the largest number of customers.

However, all ruthless marketers are relentless. You must develop the heart of the lion and the mind of the fox! You must be bold and audacious — and a bit cunning in order to seize the greatest opportunities for sales and profits.

It's not about lying to people or cheating them — but it is about mastering the art of getting the largest number of people in your market to give you the largest amount of their disposable income!

The Truth about Ruthless Marketing

Despite the name, ruthless marketing has nothing to do with ripping people off. **Ruthless marketing is simply about extracting the largest amount of sales and profits from your target marketplace that you legally and morally can.** To do this, you must reach out to the largest number of customers. You've got to develop the heart of the lion, the mind of the fox. **Ruthless marketers are relentless.** You've got to be bold, audacious, and cunning in order to seize the greatest opportunities for sales and profits.

Again, it's *not* about lying to people, or cheating them. It's about mastering the art of getting the largest number of people in your market to give you the largest amount of their disposable income on a regular basis. We've published several books now with "Ruthless Marketing" in the title, but we don't necessarily use the term "ruthless" the way some people do. If you take a look at the dictionary definition, you'll see that *ruthless* is an old word from the 16th century. It's not necessarily a good word, since by its original definition it means being able to hurt people without feeling any remorse, like a sociopath might. People who are ruthless in that sense are going to screw you around, no matter what. They're not going to feel any guilt about it; in fact, they might even feel good about it. It might give them *pleasure* to hurt you.

But the English language has changed over the centuries, and now, **"ruthless" just means to be more aggressive.** So as it relates to business, you always have to be focused on selling... constantly. Selling is what brings in all the money. **And you've got to think offensively: you can't just wait for people to come to you.** You've got to go to them first—and you've got to do so in ways that are audacious and outrageous and over the top, because we live in an over-competitive, overcrowded, over-hyped marketplace, where the average consumer is subjected to more advertising and sales messages than ever before in history. The average consumer has so many choices available to them; and they're jaded, they're skeptical, they're tuned out.

That's why you've *got* to do things that go over the top. You've got to do things that are outrageous and bold. You have to be relentless; you can never give up. You've got to keep attacking and attacking. **Develop the heart of the lion and the mind of the fox.** Consider the lion, the king of the veldt (lions don't really live in the jungle). You think of something that's bold and powerful; and as it relates to business, there's a warmth about it. But there's a certain amount of confidence as well. **Confidence is an attractor.** People are looking for and are attracted to and will follow a confident salesperson, a confident entrepreneur. The confidence that you have in yourself, in your company, your products and service, will transfer over to the prospective buyers and your best clients. **Part of why they're so eager to do business with you is because they're confused and frustrated.** But they see your belief in something, your confidence in it; they see your power, and so naturally, they want to follow.

So think about the lion, loud and proud and strutting around. And then think about the fox. The fox is very careful, cautious, smart. **The fox has that essential quality of good entrepreneurs, where they think things through before they move.** They're careful. They're just a little on edge. We have foxes here in Kansas, but you hardly ever see them. Usually they only come out at night, and then they're very quick, and they conceal themselves well.

Having the mind of the fox and the heart of the lion are excellent metaphors, and all great marketers have these qualities about them.

One of my best stories on this aspect of the entrepreneurial mind comes from a book written in 1985: John F. Love's *Behind the Golden Arches.* I've never read a book so powerful. It's a big, detailed book, and there are certain chapters I've read over and over again. I'm going to cite a couple of paragraphs out of this book right now. The book's a little outdated, but this story itself is timeless, a perfect illustration of ruthless marketing in its purest form. Here it is, on page 113 in Chapter Six:

It was the early 1960s. Jack Roschman was standing in a Burger Chef he was about to open in Springfield, Ohio. It was to be one of more than 100 Burger Chefs that Roschman would open in Ohio under his franchise for the entire state, but the opening in Springfield would never be forgotten.

A construction crew across the street was putting the finishing touches on a brand new McDonald's, and Roschman was intensely watching the progress of the restaurant that would be his first head-to-head encounter with his archrival. As he was looking out his window, he saw a man walking from McDonald's to his Burger Chef, and he assumed it was the new McDonald's franchisee. It was actually Ralph Lanphar, McDonald's new area supervisor. And as he approached, Roschman was preparing to exchange pleasantries or suggest how the two new hamburger stores might provide each other emergency supplies or hamburger buns and other fast-food staples.

He knew that McDonald's was gaining a reputation as not exactly the friendliest operator around. But nonetheless, he was not prepared for the greeting that he got. And that greeting went like this: **"Hello, I'm the McDonald's supervisor," Lanphar told Roschman, "and we're going to run you out of business."**

I just love that story! **To me, that's the essence of what ruthless marketing is all about: *The competitor is the enemy.*** Now, I've got some competitors who are really good friends, and I certainly don't think of them as the enemy. Nonetheless, we're out to do the very best that we can, to be the best we can be. **We're going to push and innovate and be as audacious as we can in order to capture that market share.** When Ray Kroc, the founder of McDonald's, was asked by a newspaper reporter, "What about all these fast-food restaurants that are springing up, that are copying the McDonald's system? What's your answer to them?" **And Ray said, "No problem. We'll innovate faster than they can copy."** I love the message there—the message of a competitor who really is out there to *be* the competitor. If you want to compete with them, that's fine; but you're going to have to work your ass off in order to do it.

There was a famous runner named Steve Prefontaine, who

died young in a car crash. **Steve used to say, "Look, other runners can beat me—but they're going to bleed to do it."** That's the kind of spirit, the bravado, the attitude, of a ruthless marketer, somebody with that mindset of, "We're going to be the best. And we're not going to let the competitors stop us. We're going to move forward."

Just think about this. Most businesspeople just aren't very aggressive. They don't have a very ruthless attitude when it comes to winning business. **They're not doing anything that's over-the-top. They're not doing anything to stand out.** They suffer from the delusion of thinking that just because they opened their doors, people are going to come to them. But none of this is easy! Then again, part of what makes business exciting is the fact that it *does* get difficult at times. **You've got to be harder than all the adversities you have to face. You've got to be a tough competitor.**

This subject of ruthless marketing is one we've talked about a lot, because it's a core value of our philosophy of marketing. **It has nothing to do with ripping people off; it's really just a way of thinking about how to most aggressively promote your business.** For example, how does your USP make people want to do business with you instead of your competitors? Just because you exist, that doesn't mean that people are going to do business with you, though it may be true to some degree. Sure, if you open your doors and sit there long enough, someone who's interested in your product or services may find their way into your store and buy something from you. But you're not going to aggressively dominate your marketplace with that kind of a weak marketing approach.

The way you dominate is by being an aggressive marketer. **It's a no-holds-barred attitude about getting all the money in your marketplace, and refusing anything less than that.** Now, unfortunately, that means that some of your competitors may not like you, especially in a smaller town where there's a smaller marketplace. That's less of a problem in a big city; unless you're being extra offensive and drawing lots of negative attention, your aggressive marketing tactics won't be as noticeable. But in any town of less than 20,000 or 30,000 people, your competition's probably going to be mad cause you're shaking up their small town life and rocking the boat.

I want you to separate the idea of being a ruthless marketer from being a ruthless person. **Ruthless marketing isn't personal—or it shouldn't be.** There's a negative stigma in being considered a ruthless person, who intentionally causes all kinds of problems. But you have to be ruthless as a marketer, so you're not considered weak. You don't want your competitors to say, "Oh, I just love how passive he is. I just love how he never goes after our business!" Similarly, you don't want your customers saying, "You know, I like the fact they never pressure me to come into the store. I never hear from them... I know they're there, but you know, I just don't feel any pressure to visit." That's not a positive thing in the marketing world! **Instead, you want to be known and respected among your peers for being a good marketer, and you want your prospects to be reminded constantly that you exist and want their business.** The way you do that is to be aggressive, to be ruthless, to have that kind of mindset where you want to extract as much money from your marketplace as possible.

Now, one of the other things I want to make sure that you understand about being a ruthless marketer is that you're actually attracting people who want the kinds of products and services you sell. Being a ruthless marketer doesn't mean going out and getting people to give you money they don't want to give you. It doesn't mean that you literally extract money from their wallets that they would rather have kept; **it's about getting money out of the marketplace that's already being spent.** It's about saying, "I will be satisfied with nothing less than 99.95% of that market share." This is money already being spent; they're going to spend it with you or with your competitors, so why not ensure that they spend as much as possible with you? You should be unwilling to accept anything less than getting everything you can out of the marketplace.

And from that, of course, comes all kinds of benefits to the economy and to society. If you're getting a lot of business, you'll need more staff, so you're providing jobs. You may need to expand your business—again, more jobs, as well as what you spend on materials and other resources. You pay more taxes, too. **These are all rewards, the fruits of your labor, that you reap when you're an aggressive marketer.** By acquiring as much market share as you can and by extracting as much money from the marketplace as you possibly can, you benefit not just yourself, but society in general. That's what being a ruthless marketer is all about.

In large part, you're doing the opposite of what other people in your field are doing, which is part of the reason the rewards can be so rich. It's always good if you can find a really innovative, aggressive company to model yourself after. **But if**

you can't, just do the opposite of what everybody else is doing—because almost everybody else tends to expect things to happen on their own. They're not making any special offers, and they're not doing anything else offensively, because they don't want to be offensive to people. They're so worried about their reputations, about what other people are going to think; and that stops them in their tracks, business wise. **They're afraid to take chances... but taking chances is where you get all the rewards!**

We're getting ready to do something here that has some of our staff members scared to death; and I take some amusement in that, because it's a little bold, it's a little audacious, and it's certain to upset some people. But you see, that's part of what makes it good, too. Some people are going to be very offended... but I'm confident that even those who are offended aren't just going to look at this one offer and say, "I'm never doing business with them again." It's just not going to happen. **But yes; this offer is a little bit over the top. It's got an edge to it. It's an offer with teeth. It's something that's going to get noticed, and that's the kind of thing that makes it good. It's *got* to stand out.**

We're living in a homogenized society, where everybody's following the follower, where people are like robots sometimes. Even in the business field, everybody is trying hard to be polite and not to offend people, and caring and worrying so much about what other people are going to think that nobody has a really strong message. **But here's the thing: if a message is upsetting to some people, it's also attractive to others. Of course, you have to be careful about all this; you have to**

maintain the mind of the fox, heart of the lion. You don't want to be stupid about any of this; but realize, too, that the people we tend to admire the most are also the people who care the least about what other people think about them.

I'm speaking in generalities here, and maybe this is more true of my life than yours; but I know people who are somewhat offensive, but whom you always know are being honest with you too. You may not agree with everything they say; in fact, they may say things that really upset you sometimes. **And yet, once you get beyond that, you come to respect and admire them—because you know that they're always going to tell it to you straight.** A lot of people we admire in this world are like that.

Don't be afraid to be bold and honest. Too often, our fear causes us to hold back. It causes us to want to be like everybody else; it causes us to worry constantly about what other people are going to think and say. **So don't let your fear hold you back, and don't try to get along with your competitors to the point where they perceive you as weak.** You're competing with them; you're not there to support them in their efforts. **Get out there, innovate like mad, and be bold, audacious, and over-the-top—and above all, ruthless.**

CHAPTER EIGHT

Spend one hour a day in concentrated thought of all the ways to build your business.

✓ That's 365 focused hours of <u>nothing</u> but thinking and dreaming creatively!

✓ One hour a day of doing <u>nothing</u> but focusing on how to build your business will help you dominate your market and destroy your competition!

✓ That's over 2 extremely productive weeks a year of <u>nothing</u> but planning — plotting — and scheming!

An Hour a Day of Concentrated Thought

Here's another secret that's going to sound like common sense, and yet most business people simply aren't doing this: **You need to spend an hour every day in concentrated thought about all the ways that you can build your business.** Apply this to any moneymaking projects you're involved with. Just spend an hour a day, every single day, thinking things through... not necessarily even working in the traditional way that you'd think about work. Just take notes, dream, and scheme. An hour a day is 365 hours per year. That's two solid, productive, focused weeks of nothing but planning and plotting.

Creativity is work, and don't let anybody tell you otherwise. One of the reasons why so many people feel they're not very creative is because they're not doing the work. You know, if you never work your muscles at all, your muscles are going to get soft; I know that because I should be working out, and I don't. Oh, I walk on the treadmill, but I should be doing other kinds of exercising. With exercise you either use it or lose it—and it's the same with creativity. **You've got to spend an hour every day "exercising" your creativity, focusing on all the ways to build your business, dominate your market, or destroy your competition.** And dream a little! Come up with ideas and have fun with it.

If you'll do that for just an hour a day, you'll profit

significantly. It doesn't seem like a lot, and yet most business owners aren't doing it consistently, if at all.

This is part of what I call working *on* your business it, not *in* it. You're dreaming. You're scheming. You're planning. You're plotting. You're thinking things through. You're not getting caught up in all the details. In fact, here's a great motto for you, something for you to burn into your memory. I've mentioned it before: **"Concepts First, Details Last."** All you need are the haziest ideas to begin with on any kind of project. You've got to see it simple, then believe it bigger than ever before.

Here's a quick story to illustrate this point. We've got a new project that we firmly believe is going to make us enormous sums of money. Of course, there's no guarantee it *will*, but we firmly believe that it *can*. This all started with a unique product idea. Then, while we were excited about it and saw the full potential, we immediately wrote the sales letter—and we put a lot of work into that, while the enthusiasm was high. **Only when we were done did we really start thinking about how we were going to implement it.**

Most people do their implementation too soon. By implementation, I'm talking about all the details, which could involve all sorts of things. That's where most people start. They get bogged down in those details, and by the time they get around to developing the sales material, they've lost most or all of their energy, their enthusiasm, their passion. **That's why I recommend you spend time thinking things through while you're still excited. You don't need to have all the details figured out; just jump right in.**

I think that one of the reasons most business people *don't* do this is because it can be painful. They're not very good at thinking things through and playing with ideas, so it's difficult; but one of the reasons they're not good at it is because they don't practice enough. **Well, folks, you can't let a little thing like pain stop you.** The more money you want to make, the harder it gets to plan and plot and figure it all out. It *does* get complicated. Sadly, a lot of people want to make millions, and yet they want it all to come easily for them.

But again, don't let anybody fool you on this. **The more money you want to make, the harder you have to work.** That's all there is to it. You're going to have tough periods. There are going to be days when you're frustrated, confused, or overwhelmed. You're going to have times when you doubt everything, and others when you regret even trying. You're going to have times when you just don't know how it's all going to end, or how you're going to see it all through. And yet you have to keep plugging away, figuring it out as you go. **Often, the best ideas come to me in the thick of a project:** when I'm in way over my eyeballs, when the deadlines are pressing, when the stress is high, when I feel like I'm not even going to make it through the day.

So, again: Concepts First, Details Last. Business is a creative pursuit, so have fun. **Set the goals first; just get the haziest ideas of how the project is going to come together, and don't be afraid to figure things out as you go along.** Find a time of day when you're most creative. For me, it's the early morning. I get up very early and have my first couple of cups of coffee, and there's no phone or fax machine to interrupt me, and

I'm not checking my emails or any of that nonsense. It's a time when my mind is the most alive and alert and awake. It's when I tend to come up with my very best ideas.

I write all that down, and I try not to think things through too much at that stage. I just let it come; as I get involved in a project, I let things grow and expand and develop. Does it make things more confusing sometimes? Yes, it does. A smarter person would probably want to plan everything out before they even began. And yet, it's also one of the reasons why we've been able to create as many new things as we have. I think it's just the entrepreneurial way. **This *ready, fire, aim* approach is probably the way that most entrepreneurs do their very best work: they figure everything out as they go.**

Here a quote I like: "You go as far as you can go, and when you get there, you can see even further." Think about that metaphor. When you get to that new place on the horizon, you'll figure things out. **It's amazing to me how the best ideas come while I'm moving forward.** If I was just sitting on my butt waiting for the perfect moment, I'm absolutely convinced, with every fiber in my being, that they would never come to me at all. They only come to you when you're in the thick of it, when you're immersed in a project, when you're *committed*. There's that "C" word again. **When you're deeply committed, when you've already set the deadlines and the goals, *then* the great ideas come to you.** If you're not getting enough good ideas, just take that inside your own heart and head and think it through.

Consider all the distractions that come about over the course of a day, and compound that. **It's easy to see how people waste away their lives and don't accomplish much, even**

well-intentioned people. This reality encompasses people from everywhere in a company, from lowest-paid to highest. There are so many things that kill your productivity throughout the course of the day, especially simple things like going to get a cup of coffee and having people stop you in the hall to ask you what you think of a certain TV show that was on last night. Boom! All of a sudden, there goes 20 minutes of your life. The next thing you know, you're going to the restroom because you drank that coffee, and maybe you had a bad breakfast, and it takes you 20 minutes to get back to work. Maybe you spend an hour on a phone call that you thought would take five minutes. There are all kinds of things that kill your productivity throughout the day, and you never know what it's going to be next. They're attacking you from all different sides.

All these things are forces against your productivity—and when it comes to running your business, you can't afford the luxury of all the down times that happen throughout the course of a day. Some are unavoidable, and there are certainly instances where you need to build a bond with somebody, such as when you're working with a perspective supplier; and there are other things that need to be done to advance your business, even if they're not necessarily going to directly increase your profitability or bring you more sales. **Those are important activities, especially when they involve building relationships.**

But those kinds of things just take away your day; and if you let those days stream together, they take your week, and if you're not careful they'll take your month, and if you're not *too* careful, they'll take your whole year. Pretty soon a year turns into a decade lost, and that turns into a lifetime of unproductive living, and you look back and wonder what happened. Where did the time go? As we're recording this, my associate Chris Lakey is 35, so his joke this year has been that he's halfway to 70. Who knows if he'll live past 70, or even to 70? I hope he does, but you never know what's going to happen tomorrow. **The point is that productivity is fleeting. It comes and goes, and you have to have those flashes of concentrated thought and concentrated effort as it relates to your business... or you'll lose the opportunity.**

Just spending a little time every day in concentrated, focused thought on the ways that you can build your business will pay a lifetime of dividends. Seriously, it adds up; you can either waste years, or you can gain them. If you can't afford an hour right now, or you don't think you can focus that long, start off with 15 minutes or half an hour, then work your way up. **Do *something*,** because if you want to expand your business—if you want to take your business to the next level—then you've got to find ways to plan for growth. **An object in motion tends to stay in motion;** conversely, an object that's standing still tends to keep standing still. Worse, in business terms, it might start going in reverse.

That means you've got to make a conscious effort to spend time building and growing your business; and a lot of that energy comes in bursts and moments of dedication to that purpose. It's not in the daily running of your business, and it's not in the minutiae that comes along with having a business. You're not going to be real productive, for example, if you spend your days paying bills, working with the IRS, paying taxes, and talking to people who provide services. You don't want to spend your days on the phone with Internet support because your email isn't working right. All of these are things that you *sometimes* do, especially if you're a small business owner wearing all the hats. **They're important things that have to get done, but that can't be all you do.** If you don't find that time to think deeply about your business, you're just hurting yourself.

Just use one hour of your 24-hour. I know you've got to sleep and eat, and you have other responsibilities; but do what you can to spend an hour a day focusing *only* on ways to bring more customers to your business, or to make more money with your existing customers. **Record those ideas in a journal, whether written or on a computer, and figure out ways to implement them. This isn't your marketing plan. What I'm proposing here is the planning phase.** Maybe you're writing a letter you'll send to your customers, or you're thinking through promotions they might be interested in. Maybe you're just jotting down ideas for coupons you can mail to them in the future. **Actually taking the action will come later; this is the developmental idea stage.**

Again, in this particular phase of your day, it's important to not focus too much on the details. I'm reiterating this because it's important. **You can lose track of an idea if you start to think about implementation too early, especially if you're an analytic type.** Don't do that. At the very beginning of the process, you're just thinking things through. You want to get all the ideas out, and not be too quick to squash them. What tends to happen, especially for analytic types, is that you'll get an idea and, before that idea even hatches, your brain is already going through all the variables, trying determine why it won't work. You ask yourself, what are some of the problems you'll face when you try to implement this plan? When this happens, your brain will switch gears, and you'll probably talk yourself out of it before the idea is even fully born.

So just get your ideas down. **This is the time for a brain dump. It's a time just to get all the thoughts down on paper (or electrons), and let loose with all the possibilities, as if there were no restrictions on thought or on ideas or even on implementation.** Tell yourself, "In a perfect world, this is what I would accomplish." Leave the follow-up question of, "Now, how do I get there?" for later. That's the time to think about those scenarios: later, when you're trying to figure out which ideas are going to work and which ones aren't. That's the time when you start knocking holes in your theory, or ask someone else to try to help you figure out what the problems would be. In this hour a day, in this stage where you're doing concentrated thinking about your business and ways to build your business, you want to let the ideas flow freely.

Don't squash them. Don't knock them down. Don't analyze them. Don't think too much about them. Think only about the ways that you implement those ideas. **Spend some time analyzing all the ways you can make it work, but don't spend much time thinking about why it *won't* work.** Otherwise, your ideas will never be able to develop. **And here's another point to consider: you have to have *a lot* of ideas.** That's one of the big avenues of success. It's sort of like a photographer who takes a lot of pictures. People look at their work and say, "Wow. You know, you're a brilliant photographer." And if they're honest, they'll tell you, "Well, I take a lot of pictures, and those are the best ones." While there's something to be said for having an eye for photography and being a good artist, there's also something to be said for taking a lot of pictures, too.

When you're in your idea phase of business, you want to have a lot of ideas—because the more you have, the more likely you'll have at least one winner. If you only have five ideas, well, you need at least one out of those five to be a winner. **If you have a hundred ideas and you only need one to be a winner, you've got a much better chance that one of those (or two or three or five) is a winner.** Personally, I generate a lot of ideas; and I'm sure that if you were to see my stack of journals, you'd be pretty amazed. It's a giant stack. If you then saw the implementation—all the things that actually went from baby idea to implementation to an actual product or service that was delivered to a client—the piles would stand in contrast to each other. On one hand the pile of ideas, the concentrated thinking, would stretch to the stars. On the other hand, the pile of things that actually came through that process and were implemented would be much, much smaller.

You've got to daydream. **You've got to get those ideas out there and then figure out which ones are workable later.** But during this time of concentrated thought, whether it's 15 minutes or an hour a day—whatever you can afford to give to that process—it will be most productive when you can just get the ideas out, then worry about the details and the implementation later.

Abraham Lincoln once said that if he had three hours to

chop a tree down, he'd spend the first two hours sharpening the ax. **Whenever you're doing this concentrated thinking, you really *are* sharpening the ax.** Thought is action in some ways; that's why so many people don't do it. So get those ideas down, and realize that just because you write something down, that doesn't mean you're going to necessarily do it. **So don't hesitate to have a lot of a ideas. That's why I love this concept of the perfect-world scenario. It lets you dream widely... and that's often where your best ideas will come from.** Have some fun. Business doesn't have to be unremittingly serious. In the end, the only things truly serious are death, sickness, the loss of a great love—things like that.

Business is just a game that you play.

CHAPTER NINE

More Confidence = More Wealth!

From the book *Pour Your Heart Into It*:

"As I proved myself, my confidence grew. Selling, I discovered has a lot to do with self-esteem."

— *Howard Schultz*
CEO of Starbucks

Howard is right! The harder you work on building yourself — the more money you can make!

More Confidence = More Wealth

I got this idea from reading Howard Schultz's book *Pour Your Heart into It*, which is the story of Starbucks. He's the CEO of the company and one of the founders—though half the time, when I go into a Starbucks and ask the people who work there if they know who Howard Schultz is, they don't even know. **Starbucks is a great success story, and in that book, Howard says this: "As I proved myself, my confidence grew. Selling, I discovered, had a lot to do with self-esteem."**

Howard is right. **The harder you work at building yourself, the more money you can make.** Another great quote from George Herbert just says, "Skill and confidence are an unconquered army." The only way you can get a skill, though, is by going out there and getting to work: this is the irony here. **There's only one way you can really develop confidence—you've got to get out there and be willing to face the possibility of failure. Things are often very difficult before they become easy.** Some things *never* become easy, and other things are only easy in part. So quit waiting or wishing for things to be easy.

A skill is something you have to develop on your own, and you have to develop it constantly. When you have a skill and the confidence that comes with that skill, then you become a force to be reckoned with. **And realize, too, that confidence is**

a plant of slow growth. That's a quote from the 16th century that I rather like.

When you're dreaming and scheming and thinking things through, you can get bogged down in the details. That's bad, **but here's something that's just as bad, if not worse: letting little seeds of doubt start to grow inside of you.** Once that happens, you're licked before you can even get off to a good start. You're finished. Even if you play the game, you're playing it with sweaty palms, playing it horribly.

So confidence is a very, very important part of the business process. But here's the thing. You'd see all of these entrepreneurs who just reek with confidence, and it's easy to become intimidated by that. For years, I faced that problem: I was intimidated by confident entrepreneurial types who had the attitude of "lead, follow, or get the hell out of the way." They just charge right through life. Now, I had a lot of egotism; whatever I lacked in real self esteem was all made up for by that. I thought I was hot stuff, and I was running around thinking I was superior to most people. But it wasn't real confidence; it was like fool's gold. Still, in some ways, I think it was necessary to get me through those rough spots.

But here's the thing: in nearly all cases, those people who truly are confident have earned that confidence. Egotism is fine for puffing your feathers up a bit, but it's a façade. Inside, you feel small. Real confidence, the kind that guides all your actions, is something you have to earn—by facing and conquering problems, pain, struggles, and disappointments as you work toward developing your skills. **It's a learning process, and the more skills you have, the more**

confidence you'll have along with it. The best way to feel good about yourself is to have some *reason* to feel good about yourself. I know it sounds simple, doesn't it? But it's not *easy*.

It means that you really have to put in the work. You have to sacrifice and commit yourself; and you've got to try very, very hard to develop certain things. You've got to work hard on yourself, too. Work on your attitude, work on selling. **You have to sell yourself on *you*, and you have to psyche yourself up to some degree in order to do the things that you must to make it through the day and get good at what you're doing.** Most people are holding themselves back because of fear—usually, fear of failure. Ironically, that fear contains a tremendous amount of energy. If you use it to push forward instead of holding yourself back, you'll find that fear can be an ally to you.

All good public speakers will tell you that it's important to have a few butterflies in your stomach before you go up on stage. **It's important to have a *little* fear. Use it as a traveling companion.** It's part of what the whole adrenalin thing is all about. I watched some NFL recently, and some of these quarterbacks that I was watching came alive in the fourth quarter, especially if their team was behind. It made me wonder, "Where was that high level of performance during the other three quarters?" Well, as the clock started ticking out, there was only so much time in the game—and they were losing. They didn't want to lose, because there are only 16 or 17 games in the season; if you want to make it to the playoffs you've got to win a certain number of them, or you don't stand a chance of ever making it to the Super Bowl. **And so as the fear came upon**

them, they started performing at a higher level.

Confidence is something that you may have to work on the rest of your life. It's not something that you're born with and always have. It takes work to acquire it, and it can be something that goes back and forth a little. **The more you can sell yourself on yourself, the more you sell yourself on your place in the world and in your business, the better.** And be sure to sell yourself on the products and services that you're promoting. **Remember, selling is a transfer of emotion.** The more confidence you have in whatever it is you're selling, the more that confidence is going to rub off on the people you're presenting your product, services, opportunities, and offers to. They're going to pick up on your confidence and want to buy into it.

That's part of what makes somebody a good leader. In most cases, people are silently waiting for somebody to step up, and have some sense of where the whole thing is headed. **They tend to follow that type of person; or if not follow, they at least tend to be influenced by that type of person. It's the confidence that does it.** Be sure of your ideas. Be sure of yourself. The truth is that uncertainty is a part of life. We're all looking for a little bit of certainty in a very uncertain world, and that's one of the reasons why we tend to follow certain people.

Confidence can change your life. If you saw me speaking in front of a group of people on a good day, when I'm on top of my game, you would find it difficult to believe that at one time, public speaking terrified me in the worst way. **I had to go through a 10-year period where I dealt with all kinds of insecurities on this issue.** I'm not ashamed of that; I've got beyond it by developing my confidence. I still have times when I'm nervous. We do a lot of small seminars, so I'm fairly comfortable in front of a small room. But, once a year, we'll do a big event, and I still get scared when the room starts to fill up.

I made a decision recently at a big seminar in Dallas. We had a whole huge room full of people, and I was nervous. I was terrified that I was going to make a fool out of myself; that's generally a big part of the fear of public speaking. So I just decided that in order to enjoy the whole thing—which I believe comes at least partly from not being scared at all—I was going to make a complete fool out of myself for the first few minutes, and get it out of my system. That's exactly what I did: I brought one of my favorite songs with me, had the sound guy crank it up full blast, and just started dancing around the room. Now, I'm not that good a dancer. I looked like an idiot; I looked like a fool. I *was* an idiot and a fool. I just made a big spectacle out of myself. **But I got over my fears by dealing with them then and there. From that point forward, I had a really good time.**

The point here is that fear is something that's part of us all. It's a part of our makeup because it's part of our survival instinct. **But in the modern era, fear doesn't have to be such a terrible thing—as long as you use it as fuel rather than as a brake pedal to slow you down or stop you.** You have to just keep moving forward, developing your confidence though experience and learning. It's a painful reality that the only way to learn, quite often, is to be being willing to go through pain, disappointment, frustration and a lot of the really bad stuff that most people spend their whole lives trying to avoid. Of course, those people never develop the great benefit of having real confidence. They hid out all their lives, so they don't really have any real skills, either. They're average in every way, and they never become truly great at anything.

I'll admit that, in some cases, confidence can mislead you. I think that people in general will follow or believe a confident liar, or a confident person who's wrong, over a timid person who's right. **Confidence is, to a large degree, contagious, so people trust a confident person a lot more than they trust a timid one.** When you're at the airport getting ready to fly and someone looks kind of nervous, really fidgety, you wonder what's up. Something seems out of place. But if someone's walking confidently through the airport, you don't even give them a second glance: you just believe that person must know what they're doing. When a person is sweating like crazy and is pacing the floor, shaking nervously, you wonder what's going on with them. They don't appear to be very confident, that's for sure; and maybe there's something shady going on there.

People tend to believe confident people. That's why we like politicians who wear nice suits and hold their heads up high with their shoulders back, looking like they know where they're going and what they're doing. Studies have shown that tall politicians tend to get more votes than short ones. It's not that people are against being short, or for being tall. When people see a tall person, that person is going to earn respect because people just feel like they're confident. Fair or unfair, that's the way that people see those situations. **People judge constantly on appearance and confidence level.**

So whether real or perceived, a confident-looking person is going to attract more attention. They're going to get noticed.

People are going to respect them, so they're going to get more things coming their way. **That's why at the very least you need to *appear* confident, even if you may not be confident on the inside.** I think that's part of what this is all about: putting yourself in a position where other people see you as confident. **And to a large degree, you have to just *make* yourself be confident.** I've learned to do that with my public speaking. At the very first big event our company had, I had to have someone else do the speaking. I waited in the back, too afraid to come up on stage. I'd never do that now! I learned to overcome my fear and build my confidence in my speaking ability.

Again, you build confidence mostly through your experience, through just getting out there and *doing* it. If nothing else, you can overcome your nervousness by poking fun at yourself, like I did by dancing in Dallas—by putting yourself in a situation where everybody can laugh and you can break the ice. It's sort of like if you're afraid of public speaking, and you're nervous about giving your big speech. You start to walk in from the side; maybe there's a podium there, and you walk from over on the side of the stage. You just had this grand introduction, and everybody's applauding. You're getting ready to deliver this speech... and you're so nervous. You've got your water glass and you start to climb the stairs to the stage...

And you *trip* on the stairs on the way up! You fall, and your water glass hits the stage and shatters. It's a disaster! **Well, you know from that moment on that it's not getting any worse.** You've totally embarrassed yourself. Everybody's laughing, although they're not laughing at you really; it's just a funny situation that happened. You get up, dust yourself off, and go give your presentation. It's all looking up from there. You break the ice at the beginning; you just get over it with and deliver your presentation.

If you have confidence in your ideas, your ideas can go more places. They say that a confident person—a person who looks like they're where they're suppose to be, doing what they're supposed to be doing—can get past any obstacle, even a security checkpoint. If they're confident enough, they can enter a building with the intent of robbing the place. They can walk right pass security by being confident and holding a clipboard or otherwise doing something that makes them appear they're exactly where they're supposed to be. **It's the same way with your ideas.**

Here's an example. As I write this, Chris Lakey has a gentleman coming to his house to do some landscaping for him; he's the guy who put in Chris's yard and sprinkler system in the first place. Chris knows him and his high-quality workmanship because they've worked together before. But the very first time he met this guy, he didn't know him from Adam. **Now, Chris isn't an expert on landscaping, but he did notice at that first meeting that the landscaper was very confident that he could do the job and do it well.** For all Chris knew, he was completely full of it; but he *seemed* confident. If, on the other hand, the landscaper had come across as nervous and didn't really seem self-confident, Chris would have wondered if he was telling him the truth about his skills... and no matter how expert he was, that attitude would have made Chris think twice.

So when you're making decisions about your business and about what to do with your marketing, and especially when you're pitching to a client, that confidence factor will go a long way in determining whether your clients chose you or one of your competitors. **A confident salesperson will build trust in their clients, making those people feel like they know what they're talking about, because they're confident in their answers.** What I'm telling you right now, I'm confident in. If you were in the room with me, you could can see it in my stature, and the eye contact that I'd be making with you, my client, my prospect. You wouldn't hear any stuttering in my voice. You wouldn't hear any questioning in what I'm telling you. I'm confident in telling you that this is my recommendation for you, and I believe that if you buy my product, you're going to receive the results and the benefits I'm telling you my product will deliver.

A timid salesperson who isn't confident in their product might use the exact same words, but the body language and sound would be different. Maybe they're not making eye contact; maybe they're sweating a little. They don't seem like they're as confident in the delivery of those points as a salesperson who *is* confident. **Sadly, this type of salesperson won't do well, because a lack of confidence will make the client question whether you know what you're talking about.** Are you really an expert? Are you really someone they can trust with their money? Can they trust that you're honestly going to give them the benefits you're promising?

Confidence adds up to more wealth, because confidence turns into an attitude that you take with you. It becomes a part of your overall package, your overall presentation. Most of it has to do with self esteem and the sincere belief that you're delivering a good product for a good value and can make that presentation to the client in a confident way. A person with confidence is always going to put themselves in the opportunity, and put themselves in situations to succeed and to do more with their business than an unconfident person will ever be able to.

Recently, I watched a Ken Burns documentary about former Louisiana governor Huey Long. Had he not been killed, there's no question in my mind that Huey Long would have become President—and history might have been a lot different. Not different in a good way, either. Let's just say that he was far left of wherever Franklin Delano Roosevelt was; he was very socialistic in his ideas about politics. **But he was very popular, because he was supremely confident. Even his enemies admitted that he was quite the communicator, and he really knew how to influence people, because he was so damned confident.** A great documentary, by the way. Check it out if you love studying stories of what makes some people successful.

Chapter Ten

A Formula For Creating An Irresistible Offer:

1. **Pile high and deeper!**

    - *"You'll get this and this and this! And we'll also throw in this, if you act now!"*
    - LOAD IT UP!
    - Offer them a massive amount of stuff for their money!

2. STRONG REASON WHY.

    - There must be a strong reason why you are making them such a powerful offer.
    - The more believable the reason — the more they will respond.

3. **Firm Deadline — with a powerful reason why.**

    - Everyone has deadlines. The prospect doesn't believe them anymore. You must have a strong reason why the deadline is real.

4. **A nice hook.**

    - If you're going to create an irresistible offer — it must really be irresistible!
    - The "hook" is the foundation of every offer. It's got to sound really good — or they won't bite.

A Formula for Creating an Irresistible Offer

Here's a nuts and bolts formula for putting together an irresistible offer. It consists of four different points: four cornerstones of a solid structure that will definitely make you money if you can get them properly in place.

FIRST: you've got to have a nice hook. Every offer has to start with a hook of some kind. Now, what *is* a hook? Well, that's hard to describe, exactly, but it's something about your offer that sounds really, really good, something that people will remember. **It's something, or a combination of things, that makes your product or service stand out in peoples' minds.** I'd say it's those elements within your offer that are new and unique and different and exciting and fun and valuable and emotional. The key to getting good at developing your own hooks is to pay attention to the hooks that other people are using.

We've got a new promotion that we're just in the process of launching as I write this. One of the hooks for this promotion (and we have more than one) has to do with a story somebody told us. And once we tell our clients this true story, it becomes like a splinter in their minds. Ever had a really bad splinter? Sometimes the worst ones are the smallest ones. They get inside you, and you can't really get them out because you'd have to tear away part of your flesh just to get them. But, in the meantime, they hurt like the dickens, especially if they're in your fingertips. A splinter hurts while it's there, and it hurts if you have to rip it out. **That's how good a hook is. So look for hooks with your offers; look for angles. Look for things that are new, unique, that will get under a person's skin, sort of like a splinter does.** It has to pierce their shell of indifference and grab their attention in such a way that it just drives them crazy until they get it out.

SECOND: you have to pile the offer high and deep. People don't want cheap things; **what they want is expensive things at prices that *seem* cheap. In order to accomplish that, you've got to build value in their minds.** All of us sell offers, not necessarily products and services. An offer is a combination of the product or services, and the guarantee, and all the free bonuses the prospect will get... along with promises for great things that are going to happen in the future. **Part of the offer is that hook that I just talked about; part of it is the unique combination of elements that really strikes a chord with the prospect.**

You just have to keep building these things up. **You can't expect people to give you a lot of money unless you prove to them that it's intellectually and emotionally worthwhile.** In many cases, the emotional is more important than the intellect. **In any case, you have to prove to people that what you have to offer them is worth far more than the amount of money you're asking for.** So you *have* to load it up. You have to do everything you can, and everything you can afford, to create this irresistible offer. That's where the piling high and deeper comes in to play. Look at the infomercials on TV. They do a good job of selling by telling you that you get this and this and that—but wait, there's more! And if you're one of the first 100 callers, or if you call in the next two minutes, you're *also* going to get this and this, plus we'll supersize it. We'll give you this and this and that and the other thing... and finally, you just call the number. **You just have to have it! It's too good to resist—which is the entire point.** You get that from piling it high and deep.

Number THREE: you gotta come up with reasons why. You can pile it high and pile it deep, but that only goes so far. **If you pile it too high and too deep, then all of a sudden the scales tip a bit.** People start getting paranoid. They start thinking there's got to be something wrong here... and they can go from excitement to paranoia pretty fast. **That's why you have come up with a good reason why you're offering this to them in this way.**

I was just thinking about the reason why regarding the promotion we're working on now. We knew that we wanted to give people a 50% off discount. People love 50% off discounts, and because the product is brand new, we're justified in doing this without artificially raising the price and *then* lowering it. People are often afraid that's what you'll do to them: that you'll play these games with the price, so it's really not a half-price sale. You're just *calling* it one. **On this offer, it's all true.** We didn't fabricate any of this. We told people the truth: that the package we're offering them wasn't ready yet—and it's not. It's not going to be ready for a couple weeks as of this writing, and even that's optimistic. **So we had a pre-publication sale, and told them that if they went ahead and ordered, they get it for half the regular price. That was the good news. The bad news was that they had to wait a couple weeks... so it didn't**

seem too good to be true.

And LAST but not least, you must have a firm deadline, ideally related to your reason why. In the example above, it is if you wait until after this deadline, it's going to be ready, and you can't get the half-price deal anymore. **A deadline creates a sense of urgency; but it's got to be real.** Don't create one of those false deadlines that all of us have seen before! You've got to realize just how absolutely skeptical your prospects are. People don't believe a damned word you say—because they've been scammed by people saying the exact same thing in the past. **Use that as your starting point: assume that they don't trust you, that they don't believe you. Then work from that assumption and start defending your offer, almost like a lawyer defends his client.**

If you were a lawyer and had to defend somebody against a murder charge, you'd build a case demonstrating why your client was innocent—and that case would be based on as many facts as you could possibly dig up, while considering the emotional elements too. **Think about that hook while you build your case.** Remember the O.J. Simpson trial? His defense lawyers were absolutely amazing. "If it doesn't fit, you must acquit." That's a good example of a an emotional hook... and it worked, didn't it?

This is a formula. **Everything that I've talked about—piling it high and deeper, creating reasons why, giving people a firm deadline, the hook—all that comes together in a formula that creates urgency.** The more you study the sales materials and promotions of top marketers, the more you'll see through to the formula underneath. And the more you see it, the more you know the tricks behind the magic, the more you're going to be able to create that magic yourself when it comes to developing your own offers. If you can create an offer that contains all these things and put it in front of the right group of people, then if you have good profit margins and the group is large enough, you can cause millions and millions of dollars to just rain on your head. The money can pour in so fast you won't know how to intelligently spend it. **That's the benefit here!** That's the excitement—the carrot that we're all chasing after that makes all this worthwhile.

Start with a nice hook, followed by piling it higher and deeper, and then giving them a strong reason why they should take action now, coupled with a firm deadline. **Now, the hook is often so intertwined with the offer that it's hard to describe to you what a good one looks like.** Let's use fishing as an analogy. You know, fish don't really bite on the hook: they bite on the bait that the hook is embedded in. In business, the hook is the foundation of your offer, its backbone if you will. **It holds the bait of the offer solidly in place and makes them want to take advantage of it.** It's the thing that makes them want to take action. It's not enough just to have a widget for sale, because lots of people are selling all kinds of widgets; and, let's be honest, there's a good chance your widget is available at Wal-Mart for less.

This is even true of the heavily-hyped items you see on infomercials. The truth is, no matter how good the offer, if you're patient enough you'll find that same item at Wal-Mart for less money. So what makes people respond to the infomercial product? Partly, it's the piling it high and deeper aspect. **But the**

hook is what you do to create that irresistibility that makes them want to respond right away. There's already something there, even before you load them up, even before you pile it high and deeper. There's something there that makes them stop and pay attention, or at least express interest. They may have walked by the television while your commercial was playing, and they had to stop. Something sucked them in, made them at least want to be interested.

Then, once you have got that hook as part of your offer, the second thing is to set the hook by piling it high and deeper. **Your goal is to pile on so much that they become convinced that what you're offering is worth far more than the money you're asking in return.** It's almost like you're sitting across a table from them and saying, "All right, here's my stuff, " and you're push forward this big pile, putting it all out there. Imagine you're playing poker, and you're going all-in, putting all your chips on the table. You're sliding it across that green felt, and they're looking at it and saying, "All right. I'm all in with you," and they push their money in your direction. You trade and you're each good to go.

To get to that point, you have to pile it high and deep enough that they feel that the money in their wallet (or on their credit card, or in their savings account, or their investment portfolio) is worth less to them than all the benefits they'll receive by acquiring and using your offer. It's all in the exchange of goods and services and things of monetary value. **You just want them to believe that your pile of stuff is worth more to them than their money.** You create value through the piling higher and deeper, so that ultimately, there's no alternative but to say yes to your offer.

That piling higher and deeper is one of the ways you provide them a strong reason to buy, **but in order to allay their cynicism, you also have to provide a strong reason why you're able to make them such a good offer.** Here at M.O.R.E., Inc., we rarely sell anything where the value of all of the goodies isn't worth a multiple of the amount of money we're asking them to pay. **We give our clients so much value that the price pales in comparison.** Why would we be willing to do that? In most cases, you'd be crazy to give up something of more value than you're asking in return. In other words, if all things were equal and I said, "I've got this $10 bill in my pocket, and I'm willing to give it to you for five bucks," that would be a foolish transaction. Best case scenario, you want to give up ten bucks and get ten dollars' worth of value. If you go to McDonalds and you say, "Give me your $5 Value Meal," and they give you that meal, in your mind that meal was worth the five bucks you gave them. So it's an even exchange.

Well, when you make offers it's a little bit different, because you're usually making an offer containing some value-added intangible. Suppose you say, "I have this package of products that's worth $5,000, and I'm going to give you all this for only $495." Why would you do that? That's a question you absolutely have to answer, because people are going to be skeptical when they see that kind of lopsided deal. **You've got to answer that skepticism with a logical reason.** Maybe it's because you're exchanging a short-term loss now for the potential for future profits: **you're willing to forego immediate cash flow in order to hopefully get a bigger return on the**

back end of the transaction. This is how a lot of front-end deals work in two-step marketing. Or maybe you're just benevolent, and you love helping people and like losing money. That's probably not good enough for most people... but if that's really your reason, then be sure to tell them that.

And let's not forget your firm deadline. Why *must* they act now? Everything has deadlines. You can't buy anything without having some kind of an expiration date. Even the food you buy at the grocery store has an expiration date. That special airline ticket offer is only good for a certain number of hours. That coupon's going to expire at the end of the month, so you'd better take advantage of it! **Everything has an expiration date, and your offer should, too. So put that firm deadline in there, and explain why that deadline exists.** I've talked about the half-price offer we're getting ready to use, and the reason why is because the materials aren't done. They're *almost* done, but we're willing to give you a half-price offer today because you're going to have to wait a couple weeks to get your materials. If that's acceptable to you, you'll save a lot of money.

Your deadline could be because you have a printing deadline. We have a postcard mailing service called the Five Star Mailing System. If you don't get your order in by the print deadline, you're not going to be able to order postcards this month. That's our reason why for that particular deadline. There can be any number of reasons why—and if you don't already have a good reason, come up with one. It can even be, "Just because I want this deadline here. I need to move on to other things." **You've got to have a deadline, and you've got to explain it.**

So bait that hook. Keep piling it higher and deeper, and then finish it all off with a strong reason why and a firm deadline to act now. When you lay it all on the table right, that formula will make people realize that the money in their pockets is worth less to them than the value of all the benefits they're going to receive if they chose to do business with you. Once you make people believe that, you can make the kind of money that most doctors and lawyers can only dream of! Think about that. Let that be your carrot. **Go chase it. All the joy's in the chasing, anyway!**

CHAPTER ELEVEN

The key to massive productivity:

Set higher goals!

Commitments, deadlines, responsibilities, and pressures can be your best friend. They force you to do and be more.

Keep the pressure on:

In the midnight hour — when the deadlines are closing in — you are forced to make decisions.

- The walls of indecision begin breaking down.
- And the answers, which were once very muddy, now become clear.

Set Higher Goals

Here's the key to maximum, massive productivity: just set higher goals for yourself. Commitments, deadlines, responsibilities, and pressure can be your very best friends, because they force you to be and do more. You've got to keep the pressure on. Set those high goals. In the eleventh hour, when the deadlines are closing in, walls of indecision begin to break down—and the answers which were once muddy now become very clear.

Let's start off by talking about pressure. Pressure is one of those things that I call a Level Two experience, and I'll explain what I mean in a moment. For now, just realize that it's one of those things that doesn't feel good. **Nobody really likes the feeling of pressure; and yet as long as you're moving in the right direction, it's something that's actually good for you.** For that alone, you should keep the pressure on. Even though it doesn't feel good, as long as the pressure is driving you, it's helping you to continue to move forward in the direction of your goals, dreams, and desires. **You're doing yourself a disservice if you don't set high goals and deadlines—real, concrete deadlines.**

Let's take a closer look at the Experience Levels concept I just introduced. **A LEVEL ONE experience is something that actually feels good and *is* good for you, and serves the**

greater good all around you. These are things that make you feel awesome. **Conversely, a LEVEL TWO experience exerts pressure on you, so it feels bad. It's stress, and you hate it...** yet it otherwise has all the rest of those things that you get in a Level One experience. **It's good for you, and it serves the greater good.** Think of dieting, exercise, and some forms of learning. **Then there's the Level Three experience, which is where most people live their entire lives**—one Level Three experience after another. **This is something that feels good on the surface, but really isn't that good for you, and certainly doesn't serve the greater good in any way.**

Level Three experiences include eating too much ice cream, going out and partying every night, sitting on your rear and watching TV constantly—or just lying around on the weekends, not doing a damn thing. Level Threes feel good on the surface, though, and that's why so many of us spend so much of our lives creating fun, comfortable Level Three experiences. You don't have a lot of pressure on you, but you're feeling good... and yet, you're not really contributing anything to the world. **You're not moving any closer to your goals; in fact, you probably don't *have* goals.** If you do, your goals aren't high enough.

Once you've set some high goals for yourself and you take them seriously, then you're going to push yourself. You're going to be driven. People look at super-successful individuals and say, "Oh my God, what is *wrong* with that person? Why are they working so hard? Why are they involved in so many things? Why are they like that?" Part of the reason is that they just have big goals. They weren't born driven. Their goals put the pressure on them, forcing them to get out of bed in the morning and work their asses off day after day, week after week, year after year.

And then, of course, there's the LEVEL FOUR experience—and these are the people to be pitied. If you live in Level Three too long, you might just slip over into Level Four, **where most of your experiences don't even feel good anymore. In fact, they feel *crappy*.** They're certainly not good for you, and they don't serve the greater good in any way. Level Four people are just miserable. I wish I could say that I've never been in Level Four before, but I have... and certainly, I was in Level Three for a lot of my days. I try to stay in Level One and Level Two now.

So let's look at some Level Two activities. Again, exercise is a good example. It feels bad, so most people hate it. But it's good for you; and the more you surround yourself with things that are good for you, the more you tend to have to offer other people, and therefore it does serve the greater good. **Taking good care of yourself can spill over into the rest of your life, so that you take better care of the people around you. But actually doing it isn't any fun... and neither is setting big goals and deadlines for yourself.** This is why most people just don't go for success in a big way. They never demand more for themselves, so they end up living a life of complacency, and they become average in every way. They never develop any real skills or abilities because they don't want the pressure, the commitments, the deadlines, the responsibilities, the obligations, the promises... all of that stuff that doesn't feel good when you're doing it, despite the positive results. They run from that their entire lives. I've known people like that. I've had family members like that, and I've been like that at times in my life, too, so I'm not trying to say that I'm above this. Again, the way around it is to keep setting high goals. Keep busy. Have lots of projects. **Have at least one or two more projects than you can comfortably handle, and set some real deadlines for all of them.**

As I write this, I'm involved in a project that I've been working on for about three months now. That's when I first got the idea for this project, but it's only been in the last two or three weeks that I've been actively involved in it every day. I've been working on developing some sales material; I write 2,000-3,000 words a day, which I can do in just under 90 minutes if I really get on a roll. On a slow day, it might take me two or two and a half hours. On a *really* slow day I don't even get it done. I get kind of burned out, and it's a struggle. But in any case, I've been really cranking up on this thing, putting it together. I have my good days; I have my bad days. But I've got this magic deadline now. I've got to have a finished sales letter in my hand in 10 days, because we've got an event next week that we need it for.

Chris Lakey will probably help me do some of the final editing, but even before I can get him to help me with that, I have a tremendous amount of work to do to get this thing wrapped up so that it's even coherent enough for him to help me. I've got a deadline. Without that deadline, I could just screw off and write my 2,000-3,000 words every day for a month, if I really wanted to. **It's a lot of work, but because I've got the deadline, it increases the pressure.** Now, that does *not* feel good. Pressure doesn't feel good to me at all; I hate it. And the last couple of mornings I've woken up and just been burned out. This morning I woke up at 5:30, and I felt like crap.

So instead of sitting down at the computer, I just started working *around* the project. I started writing stuff down, just trying to get my blood flowing. Actually, I didn't sit down at all for the first six hours this morning; I was up on my feet, moving around. I was trying to pump myself up, drinking lots of coffee, pacing, just trying to do what I needed to do to keep moving forward. That's part of what this whole Level Two thing is all about. **It just doing what you know you *have* to do, even if it doesn't feel good, and being willing to push through the difficult periods to get to the other side.** The benefit of getting older is that you know that good days and bad days are just part of life, so you try to just get through the bad days. You put your head down and charge through.

Having these deadlines is vitally important. By the way: originally, the word "deadline" meant that if you didn't complete your project by then, you were dead. Things aren't quite so harsh now, thank goodness! In my example, Chris and I have to deliver a presentation to some of our clients next week on this revolutionary new project. It represents something entirely different from what we've ever done before. I've got about one week to really crank it out now, so Chris can help me do some of the final editing. By Wednesday of next week, we need to be scrambling to get this thing complete and ready to go. Without that deadline, I'm dead.

You just have to be willing to work through the pain. You set these goals, not knowing exactly how they're all going to work out—but you must be willing to go through the uncertainty. **There's a certain level of doubt that you have to endure—the confusion, the frustration—and you just have to work it out.** As I've emphasized before, sometimes your best ideas come late in the process. That's true of this project here: I started on it a few months ago, mapping it out and working with other people on it; but, it's only been in the last two or three weeks that I've really been cranking it out, and I just started getting some of my very best ideas four or five days ago. **Had I not been willing to make that commitment, that obligation, where every day I was willing to work on it, I wouldn't have had the big breakthrough that I had a few days ago that will hopefully lead to this thing producing a lot of money for us and our clients.**

Just set those goals. Don't worry about how you're going to achieve them, at first; just start working towards achieving them, and be willing to go through hell before you get to heaven, so to speak. **Your best ideas will come to you as you move along.** What most people don't understand is that the simple process of setting those high goals, the determination to raise the bar, puts you in position to achieve those goals. I think that's the problem for many people: **they never dream seriously.** They never make the decision to do more than what they're doing right now, to get beyond their current reality, to take things to the next level. When setting goals, it all starts within you, somewhere in your mind. You have a choice to make. **Are you content or discontent about the way things are, the status quo?** If you're discontent, are you discontent enough to make a change?

The average person never decides to be great. They

never decide to set higher goals for themselves; they continue doing things the way they've always done them, and in general their life looks the same today as it did a year ago, or five years ago, or ten years ago. The older they get, the more life experience they've had at doing the same thing over and over again. Now, there's a big difference between someone who's experienced a lot of life by doing a lot of things, versus someone who is, at that same age, just a seasoned veteran of life. Mostly, it turns out they've done the same thing over and over for decades.

Those two people have lived different lives. They've had different experiences. They've achieved different results, most likely because one of them chose to set higher goals. One of them decided that they would *not* continue doing the same thing they've always done. The fact is, all of us start out at the same place in life. There's no royalty here in the United States. There are successful families, but I think that there are plenty of examples even in those successful families of kids who haven't followed in their parents' footsteps. **One of the great thing about America is you can succeed or fail; it's up to you, and everybody has the right and the freedom to do either.**

So, when it comes to setting higher goals, we all start out the same. Most of us have the same opportunity to attend school. We have the same opportunity to decide to graduate or not, or get a GED, to attend a college if that's something we aspire to do, or to acquire a skill and enter a career of some kind. We have the ability to start our own businesses. We have the ability to determine how much we're going to fight for success. **Some of us aspire to those things. Others go other routes and, maybe,**

some people chose to take a less demanding path. Some people choose to remain essentially a baby in life: they choose to continue to live at home, continue to be a couch potato, continue to have a job that's beneath their abilities... because they never aspire to anything.

Within certain broad guidelines (and they're very broad) we all have the ability to maximize productivity through setting higher goals, but unfortunately many of us never achieve that, because we don't start with a mission and vision from the very beginning. **The mindset of setting higher goals begins with the determination that you're going to do everything you can to succeed.** The fact is, not everybody *does* succeed; not everybody finds success or achieve riches. But this isn't about always reaching the goals you set; it's just about setting higher goals to begin with, and then seeing what you can accomplish.

We have the right, in America, to life, liberty, and the pursuit of happiness. There's no *inherent* right to happiness, but we all have the right to *pursue* it. And sometimes you do have to chase it down and catch it. **The point is, we have the right to set goals as high as we want.** We have the right to achieve, within certain legal, moral, and ethic guidelines, any of those goals that we set out to achieve.

You do that through maximum goal setting—through setting the bar higher than you imagined you could reach. You do that through making commitments, making deadlines, having responsibilities. **Putting the pressure on forces you to do more, and to be more, and to achieve more, because you've got to step up to the plate.** There's no Plan B. Past a certain point, there's no opportunity to take the Chicken Exit to right back where you started, like you might see on a roller-coaster, right there at the top of the line just before you step into the Beast.

So you've got a decision to make. When you set those deadlines and take on those commitments, they'll soon take you to the point where you have to make the final decision about whether to take the Chicken Exit... or to go ahead and achieve what you're trying to do. **Successful entrepreneurs—or at least, those determined to succeed—blow past the Chicken Exit point so quickly that most don't even see it.** They're so determined to achieve those goals they set that the Chicken Exit doesn't even register.

Keeping the pressure on with goals is important. **A deadline really isn't a deadline if it's way out there.** Let's say you're 35, and you had a goal that you were going to lose 20 pounds by age 40. That's five years! Let's be realistic here: most of us would spend four or four and a half of those years just sitting back and relaxing, knowing that the deadline is a long way off. Then we'd get around to figuring out how to lose 20 pounds in six months. Ho, hum. Whereas if you have to do something really fast, because you have a deadline that's breathing down your neck, you tend to fight harder for that goal. **If the goal is consequential—and it should be, or why bother?—then a tight deadline will squeeze you to action.** It will make you pay attention to it, because it's breathing down your neck. You can't avoid it: it's right there in front of you, bearing down like a locomotive. And in those midnight hours, when the deadlines are fast approaching, you're forced to make decisions.

Now, that doesn't mean you're always going to make

the *right* decisions. Entrepreneurs are known for being risk-takers, and we occasionally make poor choices that end up backfiring on us. **Sometimes, you make a decision that doesn't give you the results you were looking for. But at least you took action and made a decision and moved forward!** So as you make those decisions in the final hour, the pressure's on, which is not the case in a loose deadline scenario where there's no reason to act. In that situation the answers often elude you, remaining out there somewhere in a fog, because you've got no pressure to perform. There's no clarity in the situation. **But as the deadlines approach, things become clear.**

Chris Lakey just returned home from traveling overseas. At one point he was traveling in China, where there's heavy smog. It's really interesting flying there, because this smog is so thick it's hard to imagine how the pilots deal with it. But I can imagine the situation as they cut through this smog. You fly at something like 37,000 feet when you're cruising for the 13-hour flight from the States over to China. As you get closer to the city of Beijing, you start the descent, and you've got real clouds and you get through those—and then you have smog. It's so thick it's like soup. You can't see anything.

As you approach the runway, you realize that the pilots know that the runway is there in front of them somewhere, given what the instruments are telling them, but they can't see it; it's still too foggy. It's an eerie feeling as you continue your descent, getting closer to the ground, and all you can see is this smog. And then, suddenly, you get down below that smog ceiling and you can see the ground—just a few thousand feet below. Now the moment of truth has arrived for the pilot; now he can focus on touching down. You can see everything. It's all become clear.

It's like that with goal setting, especially with the pressure of an approaching deadline. **Early on, it's foggy. Very little is clear, but as you approach that goal, as that deadline bears down on you, you start to make decisions. Things become more clear. You see the target, and then you can focus on hitting that.** So set the highest goals you can, because the higher the goal, the higher you'll hit. **Now, you don't *always* hit your goals.** You want your goal to be achievable, but you don't want it to be too easy; so sometimes you don't quite hit the mark. But you need to set it high anyway. **Set your goals just beyond your reach, a bit higher than what you're comfortable with, and then set those tight deadlines.** Mark your target, and then work to hit your target. Even if you don't quite make it, work to hit higher than you would have otherwise. I assure you, in those final hours, as that deadline approaches, things will become more clear.

I would encourage you have a variety of different goals, too, in relation to your broader mission. Going back to the airline analogy: on the flight from Chicago to Beijing that Chris Lakey took recently, the mission was to get to Beijing. The broad goal of the airplane crew was to leave Chicago and land in China 13 hours or so later. Yet that wasn't the only goal they had to hit: they also needed to hit a number of different points along the way—moving from Chicago over Canada, over the North Pole, over Mongolia and Russia, and eventually into China to land in Beijing—and they needed to maintain a specific altitude. Those are marker goals, which you should also have on your journey as you work toward the broader "mountaintop" goals you're trying to reach.

All the other goals along the way let you score little moral victories to mark your progress, like a report card in school. **These are benchmarks to tell you whether you're on the right track or not.** If you have this big, huge goal that's way out there, it's easy to get distracted. **But if you have a bunch of smaller goals along the way, all pointing you in the right direction, you're much more likely to hit that big goal.**

Chapter Twelve

The real business
is between our ears
and in our hearts —
not in the office!

The Real Business

Your real business is between your ears and in your heart: it's not in your office. I learned this secret from Russ von Hoelscher. Back in 1993, M.O.R.E., Inc. hit a wall; that's what they call it in the runners' world, where you just run out of gas and can't move another inch. We'd been in business for a handful of years, and the major promotion that had brought us millions of dollars, "Dialing for Dollars," all of a sudden quit working. Meanwhile, we hit this plateau where we were testing a lot of things but they weren't working out for us. I was depressed and upset; and since I couldn't see the future, I was worried that maybe we weren't going to get through it. Back then, during the height of the "Dialing for Dollars" days, we had 30 or 40 employees, and I was afraid that we might dramatically and suddenly have to let a bunch of them go.

Russ von Hoelscher had been in business for a couple of decades at that point. I was venting some of this to him, and he said, "T.J., just remember that the real business isn't over there at the office on 305 East Main. The real business is between your ears and in your heart." **That simple concept helped me think things through and adjust my attitude, to my benefit and my company's, and I've adopted it as one of my mantras.**

Case in point: over this past weekend, I was helping my wife move her office into one of the nicest rooms in our house, and I was telling her how good it looked and how nice it was. She said to me, "Don't be jealous," and I said, "Hell, I'm not jealous. **My office is wherever I am. That's my office."** Then she laughed a little, but of course that's the truth! If I'm driving down the road, that's my office. I'm making phone calls; sometimes I'm taking notes (which is probably not a safe thing to do), and sometimes I'm even reading while I'm driving down the road. It's my office. Even when I'm sitting in front of the TV and blanking out, like I'm going to do tonight when I watch "Monday Night Football," **I'm always thinking about the business, constantly. It's with me, always.**

That's the way it is for an entrepreneur. There are no time clocks to punch; there is no 40-hour week. This is something that we live with constantly. **The business is with us all the time, and I wouldn't have it any other way.** Does it create problems sometimes? You bet it does. Sometimes I wish I could just punch in and out during the hard times, **but basically what makes entrepreneurs great is the fact that they give it all they've got.** They put themselves into the business; they put their hearts into it, their souls into it. They lose themselves in their work where all of a sudden a whole day goes by and you don't even remember if you ate lunch, and you know you must have used the bathroom a couple of times, but you sure don't recall it. You're fully engaged in what you're doing.

That's where the passion and the joy are in life, and I feel so sorry for people who are just working to get money. That's all they care about; they don't really enjoy their jobs, and they can't wait to punch out every day because their real life, supposedly, is off the clock. But really they're just cheating themselves, because they're spending a significant part of their life doing something that they don't enjoy.

That's not what being in business is all about. Being in business is doing things where you can throw your whole heart and soul into it, where you can enjoy every moment of it, and it's a 24/7/365 kind of thing. **You're always thinking, constantly.** You're always striving to work on your business, not in it. **You're willing to do whatever it takes and go through whatever it is you've got to go through.** You're always focused on new product development, and creating new offers and strategies, just constantly thinking all the time, so that it's with you and continues to be with you. **And while you can't control everything, and you can't see the future, to a large degree you *can* shape the future of your business by putting your whole heart and soul into it.**

That's what this whole concept is all about. **The business is an extension of you.** Sure, it's also the people you work with—staff, joint venture partners, suppliers. It's a lifestyle that includes all of them, but it's still an extension of *you*. **It's something you really can put your whole heart and soul into; it's something you can love.** You really can. It's a very passionate kind of thing, and a lot of employees don't understand that because to them, work is just about acquiring money to pay their bills. That's all they're focused on; that's all they care about. But to us, to the entrepreneurs, it's about something much bigger than all of that.

Even then, many people still think about their businesses in a fixed way. They think, "I'm in the coffee business, and I've got a coffee store, and here's my location where you can come buy coffee," or "I'm an electrician and my office is over here, even though I do work all over the city," and if you have a restaurant, your restaurant is your business, and you're located over here in this building. **So many people think of businesses as being fixed things; they don't think about them in a conceptual way at all, or in any way outside of the physical world.** So whatever they do becomes their business.

I think that this strategy is a good reminder that *you* are the business. You may have a retail store, or you may have a storefront of some kind, or a restaurant, or you may do your business out of a certain location, but really, your office is wherever you are.

It doesn't matter where an entrepreneur is, they can be thinking about their business. So, if you're sitting in front of a TV at home, you could be on your laptop doing business, or working on your business while you're watching television or a movie. If you're driving in the car, you could be doing business. You can be doing business on vacation, whether you're on the beach or in the city. Even if you're out of the country, you could be working on your business. **It doesn't matter where you are; the business is you. It's never away from you. You can't leave it.**

In some cases, in some ways, that inability to get away from your business can be a bad thing. It's not something that you can put down or punch out of. You can't even forget about it for the weekend. You pretty much live and breathe it daily—and yet that's why this principle is so apt. You live the business; it's a part of you. You may have periods where you're not actively thinking about it, you may intentionally take a vacation from business for a while, but it's always there.

For example: it doesn't matter whether I'm on vacation or at home or at the office or wherever I am, when I encounter a great money-making idea, I notice it. Whenever I encounter great marketing, I notice it. It may go in one ear and out the other; I may not pay it much attention at the moment, but I do notice, and you can bet that if it's something I think is a real good idea or is real interesting, I'll write it down or send myself an email and remind myself to look at it later.

Your business becomes a part of who you are, and there's no separating you from it. It's a part of your DNA, really; it's something at your core. Whatever your business is, whatever industry you serve and whoever your customers are, **the large part of how you succeed in your business is going to be determined by how you think and how you act about your business, and the way that you live it more than the way that you *do* it.** The industry doesn't matter; this is true whether you're a restaurateur, or a plumber or an electrician, or an information marketer or an Internet entrepreneur.

And keep this in mind: as the owner of the business, the time you spend functionally working your business—say, if you have a restaurant and you're a chef, or you're a plumber and you're unplugging toilets—is *not* generally going to be the time when the most money is made. **The real money is made in the innovation and marketing.** It's made in those times when you're thinking about all the ways you can make more money in the marketplace, the ways you can serve your customers and earn a profit doing so. **It's all the time spent thinking and working on your business conceptually. It's the time you**

spend actually crafting offers and working on ways to sell more things to your existing customers, or bringing in new customers, that really matters.

So again, it's not the time you spend ***doing*****; it's the time you spend thinking and analyzing that will have the most impact on your business.** That's what I'm talking about here. The real business isn't what you do; it's not the marketplace you're in. **It's all the stuff between your ears and in your heart that goes into what you do with your business. That's what really matters.**

CHAPTER THIRTEEN

I read a book on survival and it said that the #1 trait of successful survivalists is flexibility. So it is in business. The flexible person bends and adapts. The rest break.

Being flexible is all about:
changing, growing, adapting,
and moving forward.

Flexibility

This particular concept is one that I got from reading books on survival. I've got a half-dozen of those books; I enjoy reading them, and I *am* a survivor. Of course, we all are, but most of us never think about it! Anyway: in one of these survival books, **the author pointed out that the number one trait of all survivalists is *flexibility*. In other words, you bend when faced with stresses, but you don't break.** You can take a licking and keep on ticking. You're pliable.

That's the way you should be in business, too. **In fact, if you're going to be successful in business, you've *got* to be flexible.** The flexible person bends and adapts; everyone else breaks. One of my favorite quotes, which I want to turn you on to and I hope you'll think about, is this: "The same kinds of pressures that cause many people to break down cause other people to break records." **It's not necessarily the pressures you suffer that matter; it's how you react to them, how you deal with them.** Flexibility is an important part of that.

Flexibility in business is all about changing, growing, adapting, and moving forward. **I think of a business as a living and breathing entity, one that feeds off its marketplace. It's always changing and evolving, because whatever is *revolutionary* in your business is oftentimes *evolutionary* as well.** Now, let me explain that. I know it's a nice little twist on words, but it's also a very real phenomenon, and here it is in a nutshell. Let's say you have a series of ideas for your business. Well, Idea number 143, for example, is usually a combination of all of the ideas that preceded it. Idea number 144 will also have a little of all those other elements in it, but only the best of what was in the preceding 143 ideas—so your best is always getting better, and more importantly, better adapted to the marketplace. Your best ideas continue to improve. And, again, we have to serve the marketplace, so the business is constantly changing.

Here at M.O.R.E., Inc., we sometimes go back and look at sales letters and other marketing material that we used to promote products and services 10 or 15 years ago, looking for ways to revamp it—and we'll almost always say, "Oh my God, we can't say that. We have to change that; we have to take that out. Change this; change that!" Why? Because our market isn't the same market we were in 10 or 15 years ago. You may have heard the old adage that you can't step into the same river twice. Why? Because the river is constantly moving; the water you step into is wholly different the second time, even if the river itself is otherwise unchanged. **Well, the marketplace is constantly moving, too. Some of the things that we call psychographics and demographics remain pretty much the same, but there are market forces at work that *are* constantly changing the market.** Constantly.

We can't often see it, and even when we can, we don't always want to accept it; and yet, the market is always changing. **Change is the *only* thing you can count on as an entrepreneur.** That's one of the reasons why you've got to move forward. **Success is a moving target, so you have to**

chase it. Things do change, and they change very quickly, so you've got to let your business evolve—because your market is never exactly the same from one day to the next.

You know, I like reading business biographies. **My favorite ones are those covering the personal computer business.** I've got a couple dozen different books on the subject. I love reading about it because, first of all, it all happened in my lifetime—and a lot of early pioneers in the personal computer industry are about my age. **I'm fascinated by how quickly this industry evolved, and all the companies that got into the business, made a lot of money, and then went out of business.** So many came and went. It's a passing parade of thousands that were in business for just a short while... and then suddenly the market changed, and they were gone. **They wouldn't or couldn't change with the market, probably because everything moved so quickly.**

In that field, an idea may have a very small shelf life; then you've got to be moving on, so you can get something else going. I know you can think of examples of that within the computer industry: Microsoft Bob, OS/2, ZIP drives. Those ideas came and went. Now, some people are intimidated by that—and I know how scary it can be. It's one thing to read about it in all the books or business magazines, about the turmoil in the industry and how all these companies are going out of business. It's really interesting until it happens to you, and then all of a sudden it becomes not so interesting anymore. It becomes very difficult, very suddenly.

But that's the way the world is, and this is all part of a trend. It's reality; you either have to embrace it or suffer needlessly. Look, markets are fragmenting more and more; they're becoming smaller and smaller, and people are harder to reach. **There are real problems out there, so you constantly have to keep an eye towards what you're going to do next.** Sometimes, you have to do things you never would have thought you'd have to do, like it or not.

Here's a fast story about that. We're getting involved in a whole new area for our company—one that, in some ways, completely goes against everything else that we've been doing. Now, again, I've talked about a business feeding off its marketplace—and we do have an answer for our current market. We're not just moving entirely into a whole new area, forsaking everything we've done since 1988. That would be insane! We actually do have a strategy that involves this wonderful marketplace we've been a part of for over two decades. And yet, part of the new idea involves an entirely different marketplace, one I never would have thought we'd ever get involved in.

But as I said, you have to do what you have to do, so you have to remain open to new ideas. We were playing with some ideas and all of a sudden, as those ideas grew and developed, we started to see something we weren't able to see before. We started thinking through some things, and then we heard about a company that had generated over $400 million in its first six years—and we knew of other companies that were playing successfully in that same market. And *boom!* We figured it out! From that point forward we said, **"Yes, we're going to move in this new direction while still having an answer for our current market."** You don't just grab hold of one thing and let go of everything else. We're figuring it out as we go; that's part of what flexibility's all about.

You set the goal, you get the vision. You make it something that's big, something that's compelling, and you develop your best strategies—and then you get out there with what we call "massive action" and start moving in a whole bunch of different directions. **Concepts first, details last.** You test and you tweak and you figure things out as you go. **You've got to remain open and receptive to new things; you can't expect to have all the answers in hand from the very beginning. You just step out in faith, to some degree.** To use a familiar metaphor, it's like driving at nighttime: as long as you can see just a little bit ahead and you've got a good idea of where you're headed, you're going to get there.

Flexibility has been a mantra of my life for years, and Chris Lakey tells me it's the same way with him. He has six kids now, so he's had to learn to be flexible! And he's teaching them to be the same way. With six kids there's a lot of change on a regular basis, so flexibility is a necessity if you don't want to go nuts and be upset by all the adaptation that *has* to happen. Again, the same is true with any business. **If you don't bend, you'll break.** Consider a football team, which may employ a "bend but not break defense" that may give up a few yards between the 20-yard lines. But they don't give up a lot of points, because they're flexible.

Chris's oldest daughter plays acoustic guitar. She's about a year into guitar lessons, and can play fairly well now. As you watch her play on the guitar, you can see those guitar strings bend and make noise as the sound resonates through the instrument. Obviously, if they break it's a very bad deal; you don't want that to happen. So while it's possible to break them, they tend instead to be flexible; they give a little, so they can vibrate and make that resonating sound.

Flexibility is a benefit, then, in all kinds of scenarios. Earlier, I was talking about my books on survival, and how the number one trait of survivors is flexibility. That's true in almost any survival scenario, large or small. **All the things you're most comfortable with go out the window, and you have to adapt or you will certainly die.** Even if you're accustomed to eating things like steak, hamburger, chicken nuggets, or bacon, you may have to learn to eat something unusual or even repugnant in order to survive—because those things I've mentioned aren't likely to be available when you're fighting for your life. Your may have to adapt to bugs and other things you find crawling across the ground on your deserted island.

If you want to survive, you need to get your protein somewhere other than cows, because there's probably not a cow on the island you're stranded on. You can't just decide you're a beef eater and that's it. Get used to eating bugs, because you need to adapt; you need to be flexible. Your water supply is going to change, too: you don't have treated tap water anymore. You're going to have to filter rainwater or find a stream where you hope the water is clear and safe. **These are survival traits, and truthfully, most of us are very familiar with the need to be flexible in all kinds of scenarios, from being stranded on an island to dealing with everyday life situations.**

So we tend to be very comfortable with that term... and yet very often, when it comes to business we become more rigid. Maybe we have a way that we've always done things, and we're just not going to do things any differently. It doesn't matter whether the new way works or not; we're going to continue doing things the way we've always done them. There's no room for flexibility. Why? Because we're comfortable with routine, with doing things the way we're doing things. If you look back to when the Internet was first emerging as a business tool, you'll see that a lot of businesses struggled to adapt to it, to make that leap into the digital world. Many just didn't want to bother.

You had businesses that saw it for what it was, and jumped aboard the bandwagon immediately and adapted their business to it. **They became flexible: they moved their products online and started doing other things in the digital world.** And then there were other businesses that could have made the leap but didn't; they chose not to be flexible. They were rigid in their methodology. Those businesses suffered; some of them died. Other reluctant businesses eventually adapted and survived. **Even today, you see this fight against flexibility in some marketplaces.**

People are debating the demise of the music industry, for example, because there are a lot of people who want their music delivered online. The recording industry is terrified of people stealing and distributing their music without paying for it, because they think people will stop buying records and attending concerts. So they embed all kinds of digital rights management software into their CDs; they make it so you can't copy them, and even worse, sometimes you can't even put them online, even for your own personal archives. Shifting to the home movie industry, it's actually nearly impossible, without some serious technical skills, to make a backup of a DVD. What if your kids scratch DVDs on a consistent basis and you'd rather not have to buy a new one to replace the scratched ones? Too bad. It's actually illegal to make a digital copy of a DVD to store online or on the computer, even to protect it from children. That's why Chris keeps his really good DVDs and Blu-ray hi-definition stuff up and away from his kids, because they *will* destroy them if he doesn't.

Hollywood and the recording industry do these things because they're afraid of technology; they're afraid of moving into a new paradigm, or a new way of doing business. Hollywood has adapted somewhat with the invention of Netflix, Redbox, and online movie rental services on Amazon and such; but they're still very protective of their contents, and they tightly restrict what you can and can't do with it. Still, it's not nearly as bad as it was; and in the future, hopefully, it will become easier to back up your own personal items, and possibly share them among the members of your family at least, just like you would a DVD. That way, you know that if you buy a movie it's not just for you: your kids get to watch it, too.

It should be the same with digital content; you should be able to freely share it among other members of your family. That's something that's become available with Sony's iTunes in its latest incarnations. It allows family sharing, so that you can share a song or a movie you bought among all the members of your family, across all their computers. **So it *is* happening more—but they're not completely flexible when they come to their business models. Not yet.**

Moving into the future, I think that the strategy for survival in any business has to be flexibility: bending and

adapting to market conditions as they change. You have to be willing and able to adjust, especially when things aren't going well. If the economy is in the toilet, as it is now, your business model may have to change. If inflation causes prices to go up, you have to be willing to adjust how you do business and what suppliers you work with. Do you need to change suppliers to get a better rate? All these concerns arise in the day-to-day business of trying to make profits. **A flexible person adapts; the rest break. So changing, growing, adapting, and moving forward— these are all characteristics of the flexible business survivalist.** Everybody else goes out of business. They go extinct because they refused or were unable to change and adapt.

Look, there's always something new; there's *always* a new way to go, a new trail to blaze, new markets to explore. **There's always new technology that will aid your business, if you'll just use it.** You just have to be willing to be flexible and adapt to change. If you do that, you'll survive; if not, you'll eventually die off, like the dinosaurs. **It's adapt or die.** A business is like a living of organism. It needs to constantly change, and you've got to be willing to try a lot of different things to find out what works best. Innovation is the key here.

Consider Ray Croc, one of my favorite entrepreneurs. Back in the late 1960s, when McDonald's was growing like crazy, they were suddenly faced with a huge number of competitors. All of a sudden, everybody wanted to get into the fast food business! Now, Ray was kind of a private man; he tried to avoid the media whenever possible. He was never a big fan of giving interviews, but in one that he did give, a reporter asked him:

"What are you going to do about all these competitors?" Ray simply said, **"We'll innovate faster than they can copy us."**

And McDonald's has been innovating ever since. They're doing incredible things, constantly changing things up. It always looks a little different there. For example, I thought it was a joke when somebody told me that McDonald's was in the DVD business! But it's no joke. **Go to your local McDonald's and you're likely to find a Redbox DVD rental kiosk at that location.** They figure you're already in line, you're already waiting to go through the drive-thru—so they might as well give you a hell of a deal on a movie that you can just take with you and then drop off whenever you want. It's an example of wild and crazy, *innovative* thinking. They've been willing to do whatever it takes, no matter how the economy goes.

That's part of this whole flexibility issue. **Nobody gets rich, or stays rich, by accident.** They might stumble onto some way to get rich as they bumble along and try a lot of things, but even so, it didn't happen by accident. They kept trying different things, kept being flexible, until they succeeded. **Flexibility involves being willing to do whatever it takes.** You have to constantly move forward, trying new things.

There are certain words having to do with flexibility that any entrepreneur needs in their character. **'Resilience' comes to mind. I love that word. Resilience is when you can take a beating and keep getting back up.** Think of Paul Newman's character in *Cool Hand Luke,* where George Kennedy's character was beating the crap out of him, but Paul kept getting back up over and over again. He refused to stay down; that's the image that always comes to my mind when I think of resilience.

'Adaptability' is a good word when things are constantly changing. You have to change with them. So just think about this, and think about survival—another good word—and try to decide once and for all that you're going to make it no matter what happens. **No matter how bad it gets, be willing to do whatever it takes to survive.** Make that firm decision that nothing is going to stop you. If for some reason you do go out of business, that doesn't mean you can't get right back up, dust yourself off, and start doing something else.

It doesn't have to be over for you, like it is for so many other people.

www.ingramcontent.com/pod-product-compliance
Lightning Source LLC
Chambersburg PA
CBHW020205200326
41521CB00005BA/249

* 9 7 8 1 9 3 3 3 5 6 9 9 0 *